'Dr Saroj Dube... mindfulness pra... Through his personal story, ne introduces the reader to the foundational concepts of mindfulness through quotes and teachings from many of today's best-known spiritual thought leaders. Dr Dubey beautifully shows the power of mindfulness in everyday life.'

—Alan Seale
Award-winning author, inspirational speaker, leadership and transformation coach, and founder and director of the Center for Transformational Presence

'Distraught after losing a beloved patient in a difficult operation, Dr Dubey set out on a quest to uncover new ways of coping with psychological distress. What emerged is this wise, thought-provoking guidebook on how to tap into the transformational power of grief and say yes to the magic of life.'

—Hugh Delehanty
Former editor for *Sports Illustrated* and *People* and co-author of *Eleven Rings*

'A challenging experience in Saroj's professional life gave rise to the deepest existential question about the purpose of life. This led to a committed and determined search that culminated in self-realisation. *Rx for Resilience* gives a profound insight into Saroj's personal quest for realisation and serves as a clear and comprehensive guidebook for those wishing to realise their true nature.'

—David Bingham
Spiritual teacher and author of *Effortless Being*

'In *Rx for Resilience*, Dr Dubey offers a narrative that is more than mere storytelling; it is a deep dive into the soul's resilience, joy, and fortitude. Each chapter stands as a testament not only to the transformative power of mindfulness, acceptance, and surrender but also to the fundamental truth of our existence. Dr Dubey offers insights reminiscent of the Vedantic inquiry into the nature of the Self, guiding the reader towards a deeper understanding and realisation of their true nature. What is strikingly unique about this book is its universality—the ability to speak to anyone. *Rx for Resilience* is a vital contribution to the discourse on our true nature and the power of presence. This book, with its blend of personal narrative and universal insights, is set to touch and transform the lives of many.'

—**Ananta Garg (Father, Anantaji)**
Spiritual teacher and author of *Consciousness Speaking with Consciousness*

'Rarely does a doctor reveal their vulnerability. Saroj embraces it. He shares how the loss of a patient took him to the brink of fear and despair. What makes *Rx for Resilience* special is the wisdom of mindfulness that comes from the lived experiences of the author. It encourages one to embrace vulnerability and surrender to the experience of life as it unfolds. In a world plagued with thinking and doing, *Rx for Resilience* shines light on spontaneity and being. It is a must-read for every human curious enough to connect to their essence.'

—**Ajay Kalra**
Author, psychotherapist, and mindfulness coach

'While the type of incident that changed the course of Dr Dubey's life and the tone of his clinical career is experienced by healthcare professionals across the globe, the culture of

contd . . .

medicine promotes a "stiff upper lip" and a "suffering in silence", especially when we are faced with clinical errors or untoward events in healthcare. As healthcare providers, we are rarely taught or encouraged to be with our grief, pain, or suffering. Commonly, we're signalled to move on as swiftly as possible. Dr Dubey offers a more expansive and courageous approach; healing through a present moment awareness and acceptance of what is, through which a new way of living and working emerges.

His openness and vulnerability are gifts to the medical profession, and seated deep within his words is a call for action; a paradigm shift in how We, the medical community, tend to ourselves and each other when we suffer.'

—**Dr Reena Kotecha**
Physician and founder of Mindful Medics

'It takes a catastrophic event to break open our hearts and souls to nudge us on a path towards the doorway to awakening. Dr Saroj Dubey realised that he had a choice—to be consumed by fear and despair or to embark on a journey of healing and self-discovery. *Rx for Resilience* is a fruit of that pain, understanding, and awakening. The book chronicles a step-by-step path to alchemise suffering into serenity by using mindfulness and meditation. It introduces us to the magnificent power of being in flow, embracing our space and silence, unleashing our creativity, and finally unveiling our state of happiness, which is always inside us and needs no pursuit in the outer world. This book, which started with a tragedy leading to powerful transformation, will serve as an invaluable guide for anyone who needs support during the most challenging times.'

—**Dr Sujata Sharma**
Author and professor of Biophysics at AIIMS, Delhi

'Physicians are often vulnerable to hurting themselves when patients don't get well despite their best efforts, or when complications occur during a procedure. By addressing mindfulness and how to deal with such situations, Saroj has tackled an important and sensitive aspect of a doctor's life that has a significant impact not only on their lives but also on their families. In *Rx for Resilience*, Saroj addresses this challenging issue that all doctors face but often don't discuss openly. He uses this challenge as a catalyst for transformation and provides readers with useful tools to navigate life and find more joy and happiness. This book will be beneficial for both physicians, who have to face these challenges daily, and the public, who may view doctors' lives from a different perspective, realising that they are also human beings first.'

—Dr Ajay Kumar
Chairman and HOD at BLK Liver and Digestive
Diseases Institute and former president of
Indian Society of Gastroenterology

Rx for Resilience

A Physician's Perspective on **Embracing the Present** and **Discovering Joy & Strength**

DR SAROJ DUBEY

HAY HOUSE INDIA
New Delhi • London • Sydney
Carlsbad, California • New York City

Hay House Publishers (India) Pvt. Ltd.
Muskaan Complex, Plot No.3, B-2 Vasant Kunj, New Delhi-110 070, India
Hay House Inc., PO Box 5100, Carlsbad, CA 92018-5100, USA
Hay House UK, Ltd., The Sixth Floor, Watson House, 54 Baker Street, W1U 7BU, UK
Hay House Australia Pty Ltd., 18/36 Ralph St., Alexandria NSW 2015, Australia

Email: contact@hayhouse.co.in
www.hayhouse.co.in

ISBN 978-81-19554-36-2
ISBN 978-81-19554-84-3 (ebook)

Printed at Repro India Limited

To my dear parents,
late Dr M. K. Dubey and late Mrs Priyambada Dubey.

Dear Chris

Best
Wishes &
Happiness

Warm Regard
Saroj SAROJ
9810492379
drSaroj.dubey@gmail.com

Contents

FOREWORD

By Suma Varughese

*T*here are books that enter your life like a messenger from God. Dr Saroj Dubey's book was one such. When Saroj sent it to me over a year ago with a request to edit it for him, I was grappling with a number of chronic ailments that were not responding to treatment, compelling me to confront the excruciating fears that illness always generates within me.

I rarely edit manuscripts, but a quick perusal of the contents convinced me of their worth, and I agreed to do so. Despite being an ardent student of non-duality throughout my spiritual journey, each chapter I read introduced me to new perspectives and practices. Month after month, my daily *sadhana* was to read and edit a few pages and absorb their content. Many practices called out to me, and I implemented them, enabling an in-depth exploration of my thoughts, feelings, and physical sensations. Above all, the fresh, heartfelt explanations of concepts such as acceptance, mindfulness, fear, vulnerability, the role of thoughts and emotions, or how to expand space came from Saroj's own experiential understanding, making them engrossing, relatable, and simple. By the time I finished editing, I had moved past my worst stage, and physically, but even more so mentally, emotionally, and spiritually, I was in a better place. For this, I must thank Saroj and his beautiful book.

Rx for Resilience begins dramatically with Rashmi's death, one of Saroj's patients, which plunges him into prolonged agony. Like a true spiritual warrior, Saroj confronts the full force of his torment by sitting patiently with his fear, humiliation, sense of failure, grief, and other emotions, until eventually, the turmoil transforms into spaciousness and peace. As he puts it beautifully, 'When I was sitting with my intense fear and dread, I could gradually see that a small space was created around the feeling. And this space seemed to hold everything in an open and accepting embrace. What a paradox it was—there was unimaginable misery and helplessness, yet at the same time, there was a stillness and peace which was larger than the fearful feeling.' This is true spiritual alchemy and marks Saroj as a seasoned aspirant.

Saroj's single-minded focus in this book is to draw our attention inward by engaging relentlessly with our feelings, becoming aware of where they are in the body and staying with 'our shakiness, pounding hearts, or the queasy feeling in the stomach,' until we feel the space containing them expanding. This is 'presence', that which we truly are, a limitless and loving space that embraces every part of us and allows us to reclaim our wholeness and completion.

Says Saroj, 'When we learn to sit with intense feelings and pain, we discover that they can be held within a larger open space. A space that is still and non-judgemental and that can accommodate even the most intense painful feeling. That space is what we truly are, and awareness of that space can be truly life-transforming. This presence is whole, compassionate, and holds our emotions in a loving embrace. It is our true nature; it is indestructible.' The ultimate paradox that Saroj vividly draws our attention to is that we do not have to do anything with our feelings or thoughts or all the baggage of pain and limitation we have been lugging around. All we need to do is to simply sit and be with them, and they will dissolve into the all-embracing presence of our true self.

Of course, we cannot forget that simply sitting and being is the hardest thing to do, and the aspirant has to go through innumerable techniques and therapies and pilgrimages and guru *gyan* before he is ready to drop anchor into his own being. But here, too, Saroj has us covered, for he produces from what seems an endless reading list of contemporary writers on non-duality, easy and simple ways for us to return to the present moment, to increase our awareness, to deepen our capacity to be with our feelings, to go beyond the veil of thoughts, and to lead more mindful lives.

Here is one that opened up new possibilities for me. Like most meditators, I used to pine for a stimulus-free environment and would grind my teeth in frustration when the drilling machine from a neighbour's house would cut into my feeble attempts to be still. Saroj, however, pointed out that sensory stimuli like sounds actually return us to the present moment, and so we should allow them in. We do not have to react to them, but we can permit them to exist. He goes so far as to say that when he is at the airport, he allows the mélange of sounds to merge into a background harmony that supports him to meditate! There are dozens of such simple exercises that can help us become more aware and mindful. Each chapter is a lovely combination of Saroj's own experiences and reflections, wonderful quotes and techniques, and finally a detailed list of practices to implement.

Here are some of the quotes that stayed with me long after I had closed the book. 'Only to the extent that we expose ourselves over and over to annihilation can that which is indestructible be found in us,' says the Buddhist teacher, Pema Chödron, from her book, W*hen Things Fall Apart*. In the chapter, 'Embrace the Present Moment', we come across this beautiful statement by writer Mark Nepo: 'We need to engage with our lives by having the quiet courage to meet whatever comes our way with an open heart.' And here is Byron Katie pointing to the truth: 'If you want real control, drop the illusion of control. Let life live you, it does anyway.' In the latter part of the book, Saroj waxes eloquent about the gifts that sprout as we become more identified with 'presence'. He touches upon how we can discover wonder and awe in even the tiny details of our lives, and the power of flow when we act with single-minded focus. Above all, we discover the blessings of creativity and happiness. This book is invaluable for spiritual aspirants committed to putting everything aside in their single-minded pursuit of their true self, but its easy and simple techniques and teachings make it accessible to those who are yet discovering their spiritual aptitude. No matter where we are, this is one book I would strongly recommend that we have on our bedside table. It is just what the doctor ordered!

Suma Varughese is an author, founder facilitator of The Zen of Good Writing Course, and former editor of *Life Positive* and *Society* magazines.

PREFACE

'*Have* you considered writing a book?'

I received a text message from a self-publishing company, inquiring whether I was open to the idea of writing a book. They further explained how they could help me fulfil this dream. I was initially taken aback at the idea, while many people had talked to me about converting my ideas and articles into a book, I never actually believed that it was feasible. Where would I ever find the time from my busy schedule as a doctor, and who would be ready to publish it? More importantly, who on earth would be interested in reading my book? I dismissed the idea at the time, but the seed had been firmly planted.

I am not ashamed to call myself a self-help junkie, and I have probably read more books on personal development, self-help, and spirituality than is legally permissible. However, it was a tragedy that turned my curiosity into a burning passion to find out the reality of life, existence, and my true nature. This was a journey of alchemy and awakening to a life of presence, spaciousness, and awe. Now, there was this desire to put it all down in writing and share it so that it could benefit others as well.

My experiences made me realise, with a bit of shock, how in many ways I had been sleepwalking through most of my life. I was living a fairly successful and comfortable existence as a doctor, but it appeared that I had only touched the surface layers of life. Most of the decisions and choices I had made in life now appeared to be automatic, predictive, and repetitive based on conditioning and borrowed thoughts of others. It also seemed that I was bargaining with life most of the time, constantly picking and choosing moments that appeared to be enjoyable while rejecting the unpleasant ones. While this was taken to be the normal way of manoeuvring through life, it now dawned on me how narrow and constrained a way of living it actually was. In the process of waking up, I realised that when we say 'yes' to each moment, life starts flowing with ease and becomes effortless and expansive. Each moment has possibilities waiting to be discovered as long as we are willing to engage with openness and curiosity.

We often live life within the confines of our mind, conflicting thoughts and emotions, and there is a story of this separate, isolated me. But when we become more mindful, open, and present, we discover a space of presence and awareness that can be extremely liberating. We also see for ourselves how the voice in our heads and our stories are just part of our minds, and a vast space remains unexplored and unexamined. It is as if our eyes have opened for the first time. Marcel Proust put it perfectly when he said, 'The real voyage of discovery consists not in seeking new landscapes, but in having new eyes.'

Many of you may also have experienced that while things appear smooth and perfect on the surface, some vital ingredient seems to be missing. The constant search for a future-elusive goal or achievement where everything will fall neatly into place never seems to end. My intention through this book is to share a simple yet profound truth, which is neither original nor unique, but which I realised only through all my experiences and challenges. This moment is our true refuge and sanctuary, this moment is enough and so are we. That does not mean we shouldn't have ambitions, plans, or desires. Having and fulfilling desires is a wonderful part of the human experience, but it should not arise from a place of emptiness. When we feel complete in the present moment, without any need to fix, suppress, or change it, we can live a happier and more fulfilling life and can work towards what our heart desires.

When we start living wholeheartedly, there is true joy and fulfilment. Wholehearted living implies a willingness to taste every aspect of our life without rejecting or suppressing it. We can accept our weaknesses, fears, and shadows rather than pushing them under the carpet. We are ready to embrace our vulnerabilities and failures without being ashamed of them. It is only when we own all our emotions and give ourselves permission to feel them fully, that true alchemy takes place. I love the word 'alchemy' and the possibilities it contains. I have even devoted a chapter on emotions and emotional alchemy. My experiences brought me close to fear and despair, and it was grace that helped me experience it fully, without softening its edges. In the process of counterintuitively bringing it closer and being present with it, I was able to experience a deep sense of peace and fearlessness. I hope that reading this book gives you a glimpse of ways in which alchemy can unfold for anyone no matter how desolate the situation may seem.

Another important part of my journey that I have tried to convey is that the more I was willing to face my shadows and own up to all parts of my life, the more joy and wonder I got to experience from life. As Kahlil Gibran said: 'The deeper that sorrow carves into your being, the more joy you can contain.' The more we are present and curious about what is happening around us, the more we find opportunities of awe, flow, and wonder.

Finally, and most importantly, this book is about 'being' and 'doing'. It is about how we can integrate the dance of doing with the stillness of being. How to lead an active and dynamic life, and yet never lose touch with that essential stillness and depth, which is what we are at the core. Even in the most stressful situations we don't need to lose touch with our inner beingness and depth. In August 2023, I had the honour of delivering a TEDx Talk in Pune on 'The Art of Being and Doing'. During the talk, I shared ideas from this book on incorporating 'being' and 'doing' into our busy and occasionally chaotic lives.

One might wonder who would find this book most useful? While I feel it should resonate with anyone who picks it up, it would be most helpful to someone facing a life-changing moment that has shaken their lives and now find themselves lost, broken, and helpless. It will help them face a negative and hopeless situation and provide them tools to alchemise to a state of peace and happiness, befriend their shadows, lean into the difficult parts, and embrace their vulnerabilities. This book is for anyone wanting to explore happiness in more depth.

There is no particular sequence in which the book should be read. The book starts with the chapter wherein I describe my life-transforming incident. Post this, I have touched upon various chapters like mindfulness, acceptance, awe, flow, and presence as also an exploration into the nature of happiness. I have also included simple practices at the end of each chapter that will clarify the themes and help you step out from the conditioned mind. The chapters on 'thoughts' and 'who am I?' may be a bit difficult for some to grasp fully, but I welcome you to read them with an open mind and allow them to permeate your being.

As a doctor, I have written innumerable prescriptions for healing, but *Rx for Resilience* is the prescription closest to my heart. The medication of presence, acceptance, surrender, and emotional mindfulness can help us stay with each moment fearlessly and with an open heart. Consistent doses of awe, wonder, and savouring the precious moments of the day with gratitude help us reclaim our joy, and life becomes one big flow. It is my fervent wish that this book becomes the ultimate therapy for peace, lightness of being, and happiness in your life.

1

BROKEN OPEN

*'I'm not interested in whether you've stood with the
great;
I'm interested in whether you've sat with the broken.'*
—Sue Fitzmaurice

𝒥 stared at the abdominal X-ray of the patient in shock and disbelief. The column of gas under the right dome of the diaphragm confirmed my worst fears. A perforation. In layman's terms, it could be explained as the leakage of a part of the small intestine after performing an endoscopic procedure for removal of stones from the bile duct. The procedure, called ERCP (Endoscopic Retrograde Cholangiopancreatography), is an endoscopic procedure done under deep sedation where the bile duct connected to the gall bladder is cannulated and the stones are removed from the duct after creating an opening. While there was less than one per cent chance of such a complication occurring, it was still very much a possibility, and we always informed patients about it before the procedure. Quite often, the case is complicated and while performing the procedure, the doctors have a hunch that something might go wrong. As a result, we are even more alert. But this procedure had been smooth and uneventful, over in twenty minutes. Yet the complication had occurred.

After a couple of hours when I went to check in on Rashmi, my patient, she was in excruciating pain, which prompted me to immediately get the X-ray done. Next came the most challenging aspect of being a doctor, which was to convey to the anxious family members that something untoward had taken place and required careful management. I met the worry-stricken husband, sister, and mother and explained what I suspected had gone wrong and the necessary steps that would be needed to correct it. In my opinion, a corrective surgery was the best option as the surgeon was on standby. So, it was planned for the earliest.

The surgery, lasting a few hours, went well and the patient was moved to the Intensive Care Unit (ICU) for monitoring. I had been quite upset about the whole episode, more so because the patient had waited an entire week for me to return from a conference in Barcelona to perform the procedure. I had referred her to my colleague, but the family had decided to wait till I returned because I had been referred to them by someone they trusted.

Moreover, she had a six-year-old child, and I had promised the patient that she would be back home within forty-eight hours. What was comforting still was that the complication had been detected in time and the surgery was successful. The patient may take a few days to recover, I consoled myself, but there was no doubt that she would eventually get better.

But there are times when things spiral from bad to worse. Rashmi started deteriorating even after the corrective surgery as she developed a nosocomial (hospital-acquired) infection and had to be put on a ventilator. I simply could not understand what was going wrong, and each day was excruciatingly painful. I would examine the patient daily and when her condition didn't seem to improve, my heart would sink deeper, and subsequently, I would have to explain to the terrified relatives about her condition.

There was a lot of pressure from the hospital management as well, and I found that with each passing day things were becoming more complicated and unbearable. Rashmi struggled for three weeks, and each day my heart would oscillate between hoping for the best and fearing the worst. Eventually, the brave lady succumbed to the spreading infection.

I will never be able to erase from my memory the moment I had to break this news to the family members. I was overwhelmed with grief for the family, especially for the child. I was mourning for the family but was also terrified of the consequences of this iatrogenic (procedure-related) death. I pictured the child, waiting and crying for his mother. It haunted me and prevented me from getting proper sleep for days. This combination of despair, grief, fear, and humiliation was something I had never encountered before or even imagined for myself.

The Crack Is Where the Light Enters

It is not unusual for doctors to face such situations. Fatal complications are known to occur even when the procedure goes seemingly well, though not many doctors are willing to talk about it openly. These are the perils we must learn to live with. We pick ourselves up and move on knowing that we performed our best and some things are beyond our control. But somehow this particular case left me shattered for a long time.

Later when I reflected on it, I realised that there was no logical reason why some incidents left deep and lasting impressions, while other similar incidents only affected us slightly. This is the mystery and beauty of life and, perhaps, it was due to my ongoing spiritual pursuits and search for meaning—combined with my practice of mindfulness meditation—that I had a hunch that this case would, in some way, change my life. The ground was fertile, and all it needed was a crack for the light to pour in.

There were a few events preceding this that had triggered my desire to know more about the reality of life. It was apparent to me that there was something deeper to life than simply acquiring professional qualifications, earning money, creating a family along with a comfortable future.

Yet each time I would start pondering about life, something more important would come up and ask for my attention. Thus, I would shake off the desire to explore deeper and concentrate on the task at hand.

However, with this incident my life really fell apart. There was the feeling of humiliation, fear, and despair. After the death of the patient, there was also the fear of repercussions and harm to my reputation. But the practice of mindfulness meditation and the various books and teachers that had found their way into my life during this period were my saviours. In that time of intense darkness and despair, these were my life jackets.

I was determined to not be in a rush to get back to my normal life and pretend that the incident had never happened, or it was now a closed chapter. I deeply felt that I should allow this grief to be experienced completely. This was going to be my redemption. I recall my wife consoling me on finding me despondent and telling me not to take such matters to heart as it wasn't my fault. I told her that I knew deep within that I had done my utmost best for the patient. However, this was a turning point in my life, and I wanted it to shake the very core of my being so that I could find the true nature of reality.

I wanted to step right into the core of my fear and despair even if it meant I could be engulfed by it. Buddhist author Pema Chödrön's words from her book *When Things Fall Apart* kept ringing in my ears: 'Only to the extent that we expose ourselves over and over to annihilation can that which is indestructible be found in us.' I was determined to find out what was indestructible, or simply get annihilated in the process.

From the time I can recall most of my life—and I suspect this is true for most people—I have been at the mercy of external situations. If the circumstances were favourable, I was happy and felt blessed, but if I encountered a particularly rough patch or was struck by misfortune, all I could do was hope and pray for things to improve soon. Until then, I had no alternative but to bear the ordeal with as much grace as I could summon.

While this had earlier been acceptable, at this juncture it seemed that if this was what we called life, it was just a game of chance. If the dice was loaded in our favour, life was a piece of cake, but if our situation was unfavourable, then we were helpless in the face of it.

So, did it all eventually boil down to fate, stars, or astrology? I wanted to know the answer at all costs. If this was how the game of life was to be played, then I was willing to give it my best shot. But through the practice of mindfulness and meditation, I had a few glimpses of a reality that was not dependant on external situations. The non-duality teachings had provided me with the idea that both life and our true nature were vaster and more expansive than we realised. I remembered the words of Albert Camus: 'In the midst of winter, I found there was, within me, an invincible summer.'

But the glimpse of that summer could only be experienced by diving deep into the core of my pain and broken heart. I had to surrender to the fear and darkness. But did I have the courage to see it through or would I get blown away from the path?

Accepting the Unacceptable

Author and spiritual teacher Eckhart Tolle wrote in his masterpiece, *The Power of Now*, 'Acceptance of the unacceptable is the greatest source of grace in this world.' This was what that was happening to me. I simply could not accept my reality. I could not come to terms with my pain and suffering. Nor could I get comfortable with the despair and suffering indirectly inflicted on another family through an implacable fate where I was the orchestrator. I felt personally responsible for the incident and the guilt intensified the trauma even more, which made the entire situation even more unacceptable to me.

The Peace that Passes All Understanding

I would sit to face all these feelings bottled up within me. The fear of repercussions, the guilt, the desire for the outcome to have been different, the terror, and the humiliation. This humiliation was more a fabric of my imagination that created thoughts of what my colleagues must be thinking about me and my skills.

There was no escaping from these feelings not because there was no way to distract myself; I simply did not want to stop thinking about it. I desperately wanted to possess the courage to be open to all my feelings because, intuitively, I felt that only by being open and present I could heal. However, after sitting with my feelings daily, one day I noticed a small shift. I could feel the lightness of presence.

When I was sitting with my intense fear and dread, I could see that a small space was created around these feelings. This space seemed to hold everything in an accepting embrace. Yes, there was fear, despair, and terror, but it did not seem suffocating or overwhelming anymore. Soon, this space began to become bigger over time, giving a feeling of stillness and peace within. What a paradox it was . . . there was unimaginable misery and hopelessness, yet, simultaneously, there was stillness and peace that was larger than the feeling of fear.

This was indeed a life-transforming revelation for me. It made me realise that whatever happened on the surface, I was held safely by a warm embrace. It was only after surrendering to the deep despair and letting go of all hopes and desires that I felt a light glowing inside. What could I call this? Was it the presence of the universe or God? All I knew was that in this journey with death I had encountered that which was invincible and indestructible.

When we gain access to this vast presence, there is something transformative and healing. We know that whatever the external situation may be, there is an unshakeable background of stillness and peace—the peace that passes all understanding.

In this journey of life all of us are going to experience moments of heartbreak and loss. No one is immune to it. It can be the dissolution of marriage, a sudden devastating illness, death of a close family member, loss of a job, or financial disaster. When we read the newspapers or listen to the news, we come across huge tragedies on a daily basis that has destroyed a family somewhere.

In my locality, a few months ago, there had been the tragedy of a child who had got electrocuted while playing and died instantly. Another family of four met with a fatal accident, leaving only one survivor. I would sometimes wonder how were the survivors feeling? How on earth could they survive such a calamity?

I find we are far braver than we give ourselves credit for. There is a tremendous amount of resilience in all of us. However, I am also convinced that there is a difference between overcoming a trauma or catastrophe, resiliently getting on with life, and being shattered and having your heart broken open.

Being broken is almost always an act of grace because it can be a portal to something transformative, vast, and irreversible. We may not always be able to accept it gracefully at the time of its occurrence. It is only later that we may realise its life-changing impact. This is what happened to me. I understood it fully much after this incident had occurred. At the time I did feel this incident was here to teach me something unforgettable, but I did not know whether I would be brave enough to bear it.

Twice Born

Elizabeth Lesser, bestselling author and co-founder of Omega Institute, an education and retreat centre focusing on health, wellness, and spirituality, quotes the American philosopher, historian, and psychologist, William James, in her book, *Broken Apart*. She says that there were broadly two kinds of people in this world: Once born and twice born.

Elizabeth describes once-born people as those who do not stray from the familiar territory of who they think they are and what is expected of them. They have no desire to learn something new from life's darker lessons, preferring to stay with what is safe and acceptable. Despite nudges of the soul from time to time, they quietly shut the voices from within and continue with their lives as if nothing had happened.

In contrast, a twice-born person pays attention when the soul pokes its head through the clouds of a half-lived life. Whether by choice or a calamity—mostly the latter—the twice-born makes mistakes, suffers loss, and confronts that which needs change within to live a more genuine life. While once-born people deny or bitterly resign to the unpredictable changes of real life, twice-borns use adversity for awakening. Betrayal, illness, divorce, death, loss of job, or reputation. All of these can function as initiations into a deeper and more meaningful life.

When I look back, I recognise that by an act of grace I can consider myself blessed to have been twice born. It involves walking through fire, a fire that will burn and scorch but not consume. There have been several milestones in my life—becoming a doctor, getting married, becoming a father—but can anything be more significant than being twice born? As the renowned American writer and humourist Mark Twain said: 'The two most important days in your life are the day you are born and the day you find out why.' There's nothing more profound in life than awakening to your true essence and discovering that you are far greater than you ever imagined.

Pema Chödrön urges us to 'begin with a broken heart' in her wonderful book *Welcoming the Unwelcome*. She writes that shielding ourselves from our own vulnerability cuts us off from the full experience of life. By accepting our vulnerability, we come to embrace all aspects of our inexhaustibly rich lives. We can touch into our core by allowing ourselves to experience our raw feelings and the raw pain without getting lost in the storylines.

How does it feel to stay with the shakiness of a broken heart? The racing of an anxious heart? The rumbling stomach? The feeling of impending doom? Sticking with the uncertainty, relaxing with the chaos, staying with the raw feeling of pain and terror, and allowing this to pierce our hearts? It may sound terrifying, but she assures us that being brave enough to touch this tender point serves to wake our hearts. Once we embark on this fearless journey, we gradually increase our capacity to be present with our pain and suffering, and through that we learn to be present for others.

Groundlessness and Finding Myself

How should we respond when all our certainties crumble? How should we react when the ground is suddenly taken from beneath us? How do we stand up when all our illusions of solidity are destroyed in a matter of days? This is the universe's invitation to discover your true self. Explore who you are when everything you believed in has been destroyed. These were the questions I was grappling with for a few months in the aftermath of the incident. The image I had carefully built that had long defined me as an proficient and skilled gastroenterologist had suffered a huge blow. I found myself questioning my very essence. If this image lay shattered, was there a more profound aspect of my identity beyond the persona of a doctor that I had dedicated years to crafting?

I did not realise it then, but the state of not knowing can be potent and powerful. As Eckhart Tolle put it eloquently: 'When you become comfortable with uncertainty, infinite possibilities open up in your life.' However, while it is happening, it seems like an unknown place where we are unwilling to move forward. I fought hard to try to hold on to what seemed certain and predictable.

I remember Pema Chödrön musing that when her marriage came to an end, she struggled to maintain some solidity in life. However, she was later grateful that her marriage had failed. We desperately try to hold on to the ground beneath our feet to prevent ourselves from feeling we are in free fall. During those weeks the ground was continuously slipping beneath my feet, despite all my attempts to keep a firm footing. Today, I am grateful for it, because it was only the sheer terror of groundlessness that allowed the light to enter. In that state of groundlessness and not knowing, I had discovered the true potential of my presence and being.

One can never underestimate the mysterious and transformational power of grief that is met with compassion and openness to expand our hearts and generate lives of greater depth and meaning. When we are ripped open by loss and grief, it serves to wake us from life's trance. Author Jeffrey Rubin suggests that embracing profound grief can wake us from our complacency and urge us to live wholeheartedly and with sincerity.

Gratitude for Life

Most of us tend to take our family and health for granted. Only when things go wrong do we realise their value. Dr Sujata Sharma, an Indian structural biologist, biophysicist, and a professor at the Department of Biophysics of the All India Institute of Medical Sciences, Delhi, talks about how the disease of Guillain Bare syndrome (a debilitating autoimmune disease involving the nervous system) entered her life like an unwanted guest but left behind priceless gifts to cherish.

She illustrates this beautifully and poignantly in her book, *A Dragonfly's Purpose*, 'Till the time GBS came into my life, I had perceived my life as whole. But now I divide my life into two parts, before and after GBS. After my bout of GBS, my viewpoint and life changed so drastically that I felt like a new person altogether. In fighting with GBS every moment I feel as if I am being worthy of every step I take. I call it my GBS, I own it completely, because GBS taught me to be grateful for all the blessings that I have.'

The late Indian actor Irrfan Khan opened up about his battle with the neuroendocrine tumour, carcinoid of the pancreas. In an interview he gave a few months after being diagnosed with the disease, he described how he had come to terms with his illness. He compared his life to travelling on a speeding train with his own ambitions and plans when suddenly the ticket collector tapped him and told him to get down now as he had arrived at his destination. He described how unbearably severe, intense, and excruciating the pain was when it first hit him. He struggled with various kinds of analgesics and painkillers but to no avail, and the pain seemed to only get worse. To him it seemed like the entire cosmos was one big expanse of pain and nothing else.

Then the realisation struck him that struggling was of no use. It was then that he simply surrendered, surrendered to the pain, to life, and to the intelligence of the universe. With that surrender a huge load lifted from his body and, in his own words, he felt light and free, as if he was tasting the magic of life for the first time. What was this magic of life if not the vast presence that was holding his pain in a warm embrace? In this state of surrender, he described that he had full confidence in the intelligence of the universe and that it gave him immense strength and endurance to bear the ordeal.

These moments of breaking open through disasters can be life transforming. All the great teachers have encountered and confronted their inner demons, and through this confrontation, they have been able to find their authentic self. It is in this process of alchemy that darkness is transformed into light, wherein the catalyst is always a traumatic event.

We are often severely tested by fate, and this is when we must dig deep into our reserves. There is no end to the depths we can encounter within. I admire how Eckhart Tolle exhorts us to transform any major catastrophe or illness into an experience of enlightenment. He says, '. . . a critical limit situation has the potential to crack the hard shell of the ego and force them [people] into surrender and so into the awakened state.' Through deep acceptance and surrender we can transmute the base metal of pain and suffering into the gold of awakening and deep peace.

I know that mine isn't the first incident of being broken open, nor will it be the last. So long as there is life there will be challenges, turmoil, and moments of anguish. But what I have learnt is that we need to open to such moments completely, not run away from them. There is no need to be afraid of getting overwhelmed by them since our true nature is much vaster than what we think it is. Right at the core of this state of groundlessness, pain and vulnerability are the doorways to wisdom.

Practices

- Allow your heart to be broken daily with simple things such as the sight of a beggar on the street, a hungry child, or a stray dog. It could even be an emotional scene in a movie.

- When experiencing loss, allow yourself to be in a state of groundlessness without resisting it. Stay in a state of uncertainty without trying to scramble for certainty.

- Allow yourself to be in a state of not knowing—what to do next or what your next step will be. Don't be in hurry to look for answers.

- Embrace sadness or grief. Open up to the grief completely.

- Let there be moments, no matter how small, that touch you deeply.

- Can you recall any incident or incidents that transformed you?

- Can you think of an incident which seemed negative when it happened but turned out to be a great learning experience?

- Recall any words, quotes, or books that changed your life in some way.

- Make a list of things where you are willing to say 'I don't know.' For example: I don't know what my life's purpose is, I don't know where I will be three years from now.

- Rate yourself on your tolerance of ambiguity. Do you need everything worked out in detail or do you allow space for the unexpected?

- Can you remember a situation where the crack let the light in? A suffering or failure that humbled you, brought you to your knees and closer to your true self.

2

EMBRACE THE PRESENT MOMENT

'Whatever the present moment contains, accept it as if
you had chosen it. Always work with it, not against it.
Make it your friend and ally, not your enemy. This will
miraculously transform your whole life.'

—**Eckhart Tolle**

$\mathscr{I}$ woke up with a feeling of dread and foreboding about the day that lay ahead of me. Apart from a challenging and tough day at work, my son had a high fever, a close relative was seriously ill, and I had to give a lecture in the evening, for which I was not sufficiently prepared. To make it worse, just as I was leaving for work, I got a call from my driver telling me that he wouldn't be able to come due to an emergency. I tried to think of some magic mantra or inspiration to save the day. Intuitively, I flipped through my go-to book, *The Power of Now*, where I chanced upon the lines: 'Always say "yes" to the present moment . . . Say "yes" to life—and see how life suddenly starts working for you rather than against you.'

I had read this line from Eckhart Tolle's book many a time as it resonated with me. However, I found it to be impractical. So, that day, I decided to test it for myself. 'Say yes' would be my mantra for the whole day, and I was determined to see its outcome. As I softly whispered 'yes' to myself, I could feel my resistance and annoyance at my driver's sudden absence dissipating. My body relaxed a little.

As the day unfolded, the effects of this non-resistance and affirmative attitude became apparent in my system. Of course, certain things did not go smoothly and the challenges didn't magically disappear. However, what transpired was a diminishing urge to resist my emotions. From that day on, I was sold on the idea and became an advocate for this approach. Whether it was a minor annoyance or a big obstacle, whenever I used this 'strategy', it left a profound impact on my emotional state.

Later, as is my habit, I tried to analyse the whole situation. I realised, regardless of the circumstances, resistance often constitutes the core issue. We instinctively resist the unfolding events and label them with our thoughts, questioning, 'How can this be happening to me?', or 'How can they say that?' or 'This is not the way to go about it'. Our lack of acceptance of the present situation causes us to continuously struggle with it.

Vidyamala Burch, OBE, a mindfulness and compassion teacher, speaker, coach, and award-winning author, talks about her lifelong struggles with a chronic back pain due to a bone injury in her book *Living Well with Pain and Illness* where she talks about primary and secondary suffering. Primary suffering pertains to the initial unpleasant incident, whether it involves physical discomfort, unpleasant sensations, or emotional pain such as sadness or anger. Secondary suffering arises from our resistance to the physical, mental, and emotional levels, manifesting thoughts like 'I don't like what is happening' or 'This can't be true', or 'How can I endure this?'

During an episode of severe pain at night, her mind was exploding with the thought, 'This is simply unbearable, and there is no way I can endure it.' Suddenly, in the midst of chaos, she had a moment of clarity wherein a voice whispered to her, 'You don't have to go through it until the morning. You only have to go through the present moment.'

As soon as she stopped resisting and accepted her condition, the struggle ceased to exist. That moment of realisation was the stepping-stone for a lifetime of dealing with pain and resistance mindfully, which later led to the birth of 'Breathworks', an international mindfulness organisation known for developing mindfulness-based pain management.

Picture a day in your life when you oversleep, in turn, getting late for work. As you drive off, you get stuck in traffic that delays you even further. The ongoing background commentary revolves around what a dreadful day it has become, how people have no traffic sense, and how irresponsible they are.

Pause for a second and simply notice the resistance. It is our default mode to resist what is happening. But does it really serve a purpose? How does resisting the situation and not accepting it as it unfolds help us? The fact is—it is what it is. The inevitability of the moment must be accepted, and one has to say 'yes' to what is happening irrespective of whether we like it or not. This is how one can immediately notice a sense of relief. Perhaps we can ring up someone in the office and inform them that we are stuck in traffic and reschedule appointments. Saying yes should not be confused with inaction or passivity. It is doing what is appropriate in a state of non-resistance and acceptance. It can be seen as a form of action characterised by surrender, devoid of any judgement or labels.

Each day brings forth new challenges. I use the word 'challenges' instead of problems as these are the opportunities to test our ability to respond, not react. The other day I had to meet someone and was expecting a rather unpleasant chat. I could feel anxiety and restlessness creeping through my body. My first reaction was to get rid of the feeling and try to change it, but then I remembered the 'yes' word. I was curious about whether I could say 'yes' to this uncomfortable feeling.

Approaching this feeling seemed counterintuitive, but it was worth giving it a shot. The trick is to simply allow it, not resist it, and stay with it, I told myself. Feel it wherever it may be in the body and let it remain there. Don't let your mind cook-up stories about why you should not be feeling this way. To my surprise, I could see that non-resistance made a huge difference as it allowed me to stay with the feeling till it subsided on its own.

In many ways what it amounts to is surrendering to the present moment . . . to accept the feeling in whatever form it may appear. It's about accepting the Isness of it. It may not be to our liking, and we would rather not experience it, but it can't be wished away. The 'yes' may not always be a resounding yes, and we may tell ourselves, 'Okay, so this is what the situation demands of me, so let me do the best I can in this situation,' and yet, simultaneously, time we make all possible attempts to improve the situation externally.

This concept of acceptance and non-resistance has its roots in ancient times. The great German philosopher Friedrich Nietzsche described his formula for human greatness as *Amor fati* or 'love of fate'. Here, one wants nothing to be different and is willing to not only bear what is happening but also taking one step forward towards loving it. The stoics embraced *Amor fati* as part of their philosophy. Two thousand years ago Roman emperor Marcus Aurelius said: 'The blazing fire makes flame and brightness out of everything that is thrown into it.'

The stoic perspective of *Amor fati* makes the best out of every situation. It treats each moment, no matter how challenging, as something to be embraced, rather than avoided or detested. This acceptance-oriented mindset lessens our tendency to struggle, because it is complete acceptance of the present moment as is.

Perhaps you detest your job, you are facing challenges in your relationship, or you are navigating a failed business venture. When you cease to resist or view the present moment as an obstacle, you become receptive to all the possibilities. Once your mind is free of the internal dialogues, labels, and judgements surrounding the situation, there is more freedom to explore the options that are readily available.

Embracing Surrendering

The deepest 'yes' that we can say to life is in the form of surrender. When all our planning has failed, and we have reached the depths of despair, there is still a way out. Simply surrender to the universe. One may call it God or the Supreme Power or Consciousness or the Universe, it makes no difference as long as we realise, with our limited understanding, that we are bowing down and giving way to a higher authority to take control.

Most of our lives we strive to be in control by making bucket lists, plans, and five-year goals. One day, out of the blue, life sends us a shocking surprise that leaves us stumped, forcing us to stop. Despite all our attempts to control the situation, we are unable to reach solid ground.

In this state of, what Pema Chödrön calls, the 'ambiguity of human existence', there in no way out. All we can do is surrender. We can define it as the practice of letting go of our instincts and methods of trying to change the life move the way we want it to. Instead of resisting what we don't like, we begin to relax, accept, and yield to the fluidity and uncertainty of the world. Surrender means to stopping the struggle against the unpredictable vicissitudes of life and relaxing with the groundlessness of the moment.

As Leo Babauta, the creator of 'Zen Habits', a top productivity and simplicity blog, explains that surrender is the opposite of trying to be in control in our attempt to bring a semblance of certainty and solid ground to the situation.

It may be useful to list what happens when we constantly try to control things:

- We become stressed and anxious when things don't go our way
- Fear and agitation overwhelm us
- We try to shift the blame onto others by judging, labelling, criticising, and venting out
- We waste energy trying to regain control, becoming unhappy and depressed when we fail

But what if we were to practise surrender to the moment? We stop trying to control things and cease struggling. We halt our thoughts and worries about an imagined dreadful future and focus our full attention on this moment. Because that is all we can do for certain—this moment and this activity. We lean into whatever is happening, however uncertain, and accept it fully. Resisting it is futile and the source of our misery. We say a deep 'yes' to the moment, to the situation in front of us right now.

Surrender is openness, full presence, appreciation of all that we have rather than finding fault with what we don't have. We acknowledge and feel our fear rather than pushing it away. We begin practising self-compassion and giving ourselves love and appreciation rather than blaming ourselves for all that is wrong.

It took me a while to come to terms with the concept of surrender. Throughout most of my life after my childhood, it seemed to me that I was the doer who made the decisions and was in control. While there were the usual ups and downs, I came to believe that one needed to exert the right kind of effort, and with sheer perseverance things would fall into place. This seemed to be a tried and tested formula for success and happiness that I observed around me.

My academic success and achievements seemed to support this belief. I worked tirelessly through and excelled in the medical entrance exams, securing admission into the prestigious CMC Vellore College. Similarly, I made an all-out effort in my MD post-graduate entrance exams, and the rewards duly followed. The DM super speciality exams presented a slightly different experience, and although I wasn't consciously aware at that time, it was my first taste of surrender.

There were limited seats open for admission to the prestigious gastroenterology course, and most of us would attempt the exam every six months for two or three tried before being selected. I had nearly qualified in the last AIIMS and was on the waiting list. I knew that I just needed a push to get in, but the limited seats offered no certainty at all.

The next exam was of G. B. Pant College, with three seats available for selection. I was optimistic about my chances and was studying at a comfortable pace when disaster suddenly struck. My father fell seriously ill with a severe urinary infection, and since he had previously suffered a heart attack, the infection spread throughout his body. He spent two weeks in the ICU, and those two weeks were incredibly tense and stressful. However, I still managed to dedicate whatever time I could to my studies.

When my father finally came back home, he required oxygen support and injections along with strict supervision. I took on the responsibility of supervising his entire treatment while squeezing in whatever time I could for exam revision. I wasn't thinking about whether I would get selected or not; all I hoped and prayed for was to be able to take the exam somehow. I was afraid something might happen to my father, and I might not even have the opportunity to sit for the exam.

The night before the exam, I asked my wife and nephew,

who were also involved in his care, to look after my father and his medication for the night. I needed a proper night's sleep to be in a position to take my exams. I told them to wake me up only if there was something extremely urgent. The next day, I woke up grateful that my father had spent a comfortable night. However, until I took my seat for the exam, I half-expected someone to come with terrible news. I could hardly believe that I was able to take the exam and did my best, simply hoping to complete it without any major incident. Only after finishing my exam did I start thinking about how it went and what my chances were.

It was in this state of surrendered action that I gave my DM exam, and no one in my household could believe it when I was finally selected with the second rank, given the dire circumstances in which I had taken the test. The greatest gift for me was that my father was still alive and overjoyed to hear the news of my selection. When I reflect back on it, I realise how often we are under the illusion of being in control. The reality is that we are never truly in the driver's seat; it is only in extreme situations that can appreciate this fact. As India priest and psychotherapist Anthony De Mello puts it brilliantly: 'Enlightenment is: absolute cooperation with the inevitable.'

Regarding Rashmi's tragic complication, I intuitively knew that the only option left for me was to surrender completely without any conditions or prerequisites, allowing the Universe to do whatever it wanted to do. One should not surrender with the hope and condition that the outcome should eventually be positive. True surrender means being completely willing to let go of all expectations and being open to life leading you in whatever direction it chooses. It's about trusting that life knows what is best for your growth. And surrender I did, completely.

In *The Power of Now*, Tolle emphasises that one's initial opportunity lies in yielding to the present reality. Recognising that the past cannot be altered since it has already occurred, individuals are encouraged to embrace or acknowledge the existing circumstances without hesitation. This includes accepting the internal state, even in cases where the external situation remains difficult to accept. The guidance advises against resisting emotional pain and suggests surrendering to emotions like grief, despair, fear, loneliness, or any other form of suffering. In instances where accepting the unfolding events becomes challenging, the counsel is to acknowledge one's inability to do so.

These words of Eckhart Tolle were like a soothing balm during this period of intense suffering. I read these words almost daily, repeatedly. Surrendering to the grief, despair, and fear. Feeling it, embracing it. Initially, staying present and open to these feelings was the biggest challenge, but I realised that the only way out was through. As I described in the last chapter, it was only staying open to the pain and despair that a window of opportunity for the feelings to shift emerged. Once there was a shift, I realised that I could face anything with awareness.

During this painful stage what greatly helped me was being present and grateful. Each day, I would wake up with the searing, numbing pain of anticipating that my worst fears might come true. However, instead of letting my worries spread like a wildfire of raging thoughts and emotions, I chose to focus on what was happening right here, right now. In this moment, what needs to be done for this patient, and not just this patient but for all my patients? What action do I need to take right now, whether at work, at home, or in the traffic? Then, I did what was most appropriate for the moment, taking each day moment by moment.

There were certainly times when my imagination and fear would get the better of me, but I learnt to steer my mind back to the present moment. Mindful practices and meditations were of immense value, and I was grateful for the background of practice that I could put into practical application during this crisis.

Above all, gratitude was my biggest friend and support. When things reached their worst, I would ask myself, 'Can I be grateful to be alive right now? Can I be grateful that I have a loving family, and that they are healthy and well?' I would return to the bare minimum, grateful that I was alive and, even better, healthy. My family was with me, alive and in good health.

We often take so many of these facts for granted, but as the Covid pandemic showed us, each moment of life is a precious gift. By simply glancing at the news, one could read about how many people lost their dear ones, and how often death arrived in the most unexpected ways.

One of the most inspiring books I have read is Michael A. Singer's *The Surrender Experiment*. The book is based on his decision as a young man to stop listening to the non-stop voice in his head and instead to surrender to the perfection of the Universe. Over the next twenty years, he let life guide him, rather than constantly judging and manipulating things according to what he found best. If he was planning to make a decision and there were hindrances, he took it as life's message to change the direction.

Over the years, he achieved amazing success and started a thriving spiritual community in over 600 acres of pristine forest in Florida. He launched a cutting-edge software package that transformed the medical industry and subsequently became the CEO of a billion-dollar public company, whose achievements are archived in the Smithsonian Institution. He recounted his life experiences in his two books, *The Untethered Soul* and *The Surrender Experiment*, both of which became *New York Times* bestsellers and have influenced millions of people. His life and books are testimonials to the magic that is available in surrendered action and the innate perfection of the Universe.

Engaging With Life

Over the past few years, I have found deep inspiration in the teachings of American poet and spiritual adviser Mark Nepo, who urges us to approach life with an open heart. During a podcast conversation with Tami Simon on 'Insights at the Edge', he uses the analogy of a fish's gills to illustrate his point. He says that fish constantly move through water not merely to reach a destination or with a particular agenda but to keep engaging in their natural environment; otherwise they would die.

The metaphor, according to Mark Nepo, is for us humans wherein our hearts are our gills. We need to move through the water of our experiences to thrive. He eloquently explains that we need to embrace whatever comes our way with quiet courage and an open heart. I found his words incredibly moving and deeply inspiring. While there may be incidents in our lives and the world around us that may temporarily close our hearts, just as a fish's gills learn to extract what they need, we can do the same. When our hearts remain open and receptive to each unfolding moment, we can navigate our way through life with courage, compassion, and kindness. When we embrace life with open hearts, we say 'yes' to whatever form life may take.

As spiritual teacher Adyashanti eloquently states, 'There is a very simple secret to be happy. Just let go of the demand on this moment.' When we demand that the present be a certain way, we miss the fluidity of the moment itself. Our thoughts and demands create inner resistance and struggle. The roots of our suffering lie in our desire to control and manipulate life.

Since we have learnt to navigate life in this manner from childhood, it is not easy to shift to a different mindset. However, take a moment to reflect and introspect and see whether the desire to control things make your happy and feel at peace. Or does the acceptance and non-resistance brings you at ease? If we are willing to relinquish the driver's seat, we can experience the lightness and joy of the journey. American writer Byron Katie summarises it perfectly: 'If you want real control, drop the illusion of control. Let life live you. It does anyway.'

Practices

- Practise saying 'Yes' to different situations in your life. It may be as simple as the house help or driver not coming in to work or dealing with an unpleasant situation.

- Practise surrender in your everyday life. When you are stuck in traffic, just sit back and surrender to what is happening. Do what is necessary, such as making phone calls, and thereafter simply let go.

- Let go of judgement and playing the blame game. See if it is possible to not judge something or someone. Notice how you feel within you when you stop blaming others. Also, notice how you feel when you criticise or blame someone.

- Be attentive when resistance emerges. Say to yourself, 'Here is resistance.' Practise letting go of it for a few seconds simply by saying 'yes'.

- Can you stay with resistance by allowing it? For instance, your resistance to the fact that you are not earning enough? Can you also find something to be grateful for in it, such as your continued good health to work or the possibility of finding another job? See if this dissolves the resistance, allowing you to say 'yes'.

- Notice how your body feels when you say 'yes' vs 'no'. Is there contraction or relaxation, tightening or expansiveness? Which feels lighter and more peaceful?

- Practise allowing everything to be as it is for five or ten minutes. Allow your situation, internal or external, to remain precisely as it is without attempting to change anything.

- Can you practise welcoming everything in your experience? Any thought, any emotion, any sensation—is it possible to simply welcome it and allow it? Instead of categorising a moment as good, bad, or boring, just let it be.

- Take any situation and see if you can distinguish between primary and secondary suffering. For example, primary suffering may arise from being stuck in traffic. Secondary suffering includes all the stories your mind creates, such as feeling overworked and believing no one understands your problems.

- Create a list of a few situations in your life where you can practise surrender. This may occur in your personal life, dealing with your spouse and children, where certain aspects cannot be changed. How would it feel to yield to them and surrender?

- How often do you prefer to have control over situations? Can you attempt to release control of things for a moment? How would you feel if you let go of control? Would you feel lighter or burdened? Observe how frequently you desire things to be different from the way they are—a little cooler, a tad warmer, a bit more organised. Simply take notice of how often this happens in a day.

3

THE POWER OF NOW

'May I meet this moment fully. May I meet it as a friend.'
—**Sylvia Boorstein**

It was a minor incident, but it stuck in my memory for a long time. It occurred during my rigorous gastroenterology training days when I was in a perpetually harried state. I was in my professor's chamber where he was dictating a few lines to me. I was feeling quite despondent and low because it was a weekend, and I was on call, so I had to spend the next thirty-six hours in the hospital on duty while my school friends were planning a party. On top of that, there was an important presentation on Monday, and I could already predict that the outcome was going to be disastrous due to my lack of preparation time.

Nevertheless, I shifted my focus from these gloomy thoughts and attentively transcribed my professor's words, subconsciously hoping that completing this task would earn me his approval. As it was almost finished, my professor remarked, 'It's such a joy to watch you write so neatly and meticulously.' I was taken aback and overjoyed by this unexpected praise.

The incident immediately came to mind when I first heard of mindfulness and being present. I understood that somehow my state of presence and mindfulness while performing that small task had been conveyed to my professor that day, prompting his comment. It can be a delight to watch anyone perform a task with complete presence, regardless of the nature of the work, and that is the essence of mindfulness.

My journey to mindfulness began when I read *The Power of Now* by Eckhart Tolle several years ago. It was a stunning revelation when I realised how little I lived in the present. I considered myself to be of above-average intelligence, fairly confident, emotionally stable, and somewhat successful in life. However, as I read the book, I understood that not being present does not hinder one's success or efficiency, and perhaps, that is why we often underestimate its importance. We might be talking to someone and thinking about the next task, having breakfast while on the phone and planning meetings, or at work or in a meeting while thinking about dinner. All of these actions are considered normal. After all, multitasking is regarded as a sign of achievement, proactivity, and dynamism. We often flaunt our busyness and lack of time as badges of achievement.

Not being in the present is a kind of epidemic. Most of the time, we use the present moment merely as a stepping stone to some other more desirable moment. As Eckhart Tolle brilliantly explains in his book, we often view the present moment as an obstacle that needs to be overcome in order to reach a more significant moment. We all accept this future-oriented or non-present mindset as normal.

Jon Kabat-Zinn, who has played a pivotal role in promoting mindfulness over the last four decades, defined mindfulness as purposefully being aware of the present in a non-judgemental manner. You might wonder why being mindful and present is such a significant issue when we can carry on with all our activities without being fully present?

Let's delve into mindfulness in detail, and hopefully, it will emphasise why it is such an important component of our well-being.

Auto Pilot vs Awareness

When we talk about being aware, we may initially think there is nothing special about awareness, as everything we do daily—such as hearing, talking, and even reading this page— is because we are conscious and aware. However, if we delve deeper, we realise that most of the time we go about our day on autopilot mode. Our actions become mechanical, performed without close attention. After mastering the skill of driving a car, we become unaware of using the steering wheel, gear, or brakes. Mindfulness entails bringing awareness to whatever we are doing at this moment, no matter how important or mundane the activity may be.

As we become more aware, we also recognise that we often treat the present moment as an obstacle that stands in the way of reaching the next, seemingly more important, moment. For instance, if you are waiting for a delayed plane, you may resist the time spent waiting, yearning for the moment of boarding the plane and finally taking off for your destination, which seems far more important. Through mindfulness, we bring awareness and acceptance to the present moment as it is. We attempt to fix or change this moment; instead we accept it unconditionally in whatever form it presents itself.

This does not mean that we cannot take action that is necessary and appropriate for the moment. For example, if my tire has a puncture, I will certainly stop and change it, or if there is an illness, I will seek treatment. However, our first step is to accept the isness of the present moment. Through this acceptance, we develop non-resistance and ease towards this moment.

Resistance primarily arises from the mind's constant need to judge, criticise, or find fault with things. Most of the time, this is a futile and exhausting process because the mind attempts to find fault with the isness of things. We must realise that things are the way they are, and even for them to change, we must first accept them in their current form.

Embodied Presence

We also notice something vital: Our minds are often disconnected from our bodies. This means we fail to realise how often we get lost in our thoughts, unaware of what's happening within our bodies. Most of the time, we operate from the upper storey, and the body merely becomes a vehicle to transport the mind from one place to another.

In the short story, *A Painful Case*, Irish author James Joyce describes the character Mr Duffy as living a short distance away from his body. It may sound funny, but it is the story of our lives. Lost in the past or future, we stop living in our bodies, which are firmly anchored in the present. Mindfulness involves the process of returning to the body and fully inhabiting it. We learn to return to our true home— our body—and completely ground ourselves in the present moment. Mindfulness embodies presence and is the process of aligning our minds and bodies to function in harmony.

It is true that the more academic, technical, and cerebral we become in our professions and lives, the more we lose touch with our bodies. Since we spend a large portion of our work immersed in our thoughts, we give it more importance, resulting in the neglect of the precious wisdom of our bodies. We need to pause and reconnect with our bodies from time to time, attentively listening to what they are trying to convey. The body holds the answers, but we must pay heed to it.

PAID Reality

Humans are becoming accustomed to a contemporary reality of life described by Rasmus Hougaard, an internationally acknowledged expert in training the mind for focus and clarity at work, as PAID reality, an acronym standing for the following words:

1. Pressure: We are constantly under pressure, whether in our professional or personal lives. There's pressure to perform, excel, and keep up with others.

2. Always On: It is an unescapable reality. Clear boundaries between work and personal life no longer exist. We are always available via our mobile phones and e-mails, even when working from home.

3. Information Overload: The internet offers an overwhelming amount of information with a simple click of the mouse, and we are expected to stay updated with the latest goings-on. Information overload is a problem, and staying updated is a significant source of stress.

4. Distractions: Myriad distractions surround us in the form of social media. Naturally, our minds frequently wander, making it challenging to maintain focus.

In this era of PAID reality, we need to find our source of grounding. Since we are always supposed to be 'on', it becomes imperative for us to have an internal off button. This is where mindfulness can play a vital part in our lives, helping us stay grounded and present.

Benefits of Mindfulness

Why does mindfulness hold importance in organisations and corporates? Moreover, why are people so fascinated by it? Here are some of the major benefits that I have personally experienced, which makes mindfulness an essential addition to our everyday lives.

Space

You may have read this brilliant quote by Victor E. Frankl, 'Between stimulus and response there is a space. In that space is our power to choose our response. In our response lies our growth and freedom.' Nothing epitomises the philosophy of mindfulness more than this quote. Most of our lives are spent in reacting. We have arguments with our spouse, children, or parents, and we react. We may regret our words later, but by then, it is too late. Mindfulness allows us to respond rather than react by creating a small space between our thoughts and feelings.

This space has been termed as the magic of a quarter-second. It is only when I began practising mindfulness that I realised that its magical nature. The situation will not change, but our response will make a big difference to the outcome. If we are upset with our partner or children, we know that reacting with the intention to hurt may cause irreversible damage to the relationship. Mindfulness gives us the space needed to temper our response until things cool down enough for a more detached discussion on the situation.

Gift of the Present Moment

The most precious gift we can give ourselves is the gift of the present moment. When we are aligned to the present moment, and our minds are not oscillating between the past or the future, we feel grounded and content. There is no resistance to what is happening right here, and this transmits into a feeling of peace without agitation or restlessness.

Focus

More and more organisations are realising the benefits of having more mindful and focused employees. The more focused our attention is to the task at hand, the more productive we are. There was a landmark Harvard research conducted by Mathew Killingsworth and Daniel Gilbert, wherein they found out that people spent 46.9 per cent of their waking hours on thinking about something other than what they were doing, and most of these were unhappy thoughts. In other words, the study revealed that mind wandering was a widely prevalent phenomenon leading to unhappiness and inefficiency. Google has a very popular mindfulness course called 'Search Inside Yourself' and Microsoft, Apple, Nike, and LinkedIn have been using mindfulness concepts to improve work quality, increase focus, and reduce stress-related burnout.

Happiness and Well-Being

As Killingsworth summarises in the previously quoted Harvard study, mind wandering is an excellent predictor of people's happiness. How often our minds leave the present, and where they go, is a better predictor of people's happiness than the activities in which they are engaged. Extensive scientific research is confirming that a wandering mind is an unhappy mind, and the more we are anchored to the present moment, the more we can access happiness and well-being.

Positive Emotions

The groundbreaking work of Barbara Fredrickson, Professor of Psychology at the University of North Carolina, highlights the link between positive emotions and mindfulness. Her 'Broaden and Build' theory explains how positive emotions open us to the moment, allowing us to take in and appreciate more of our surroundings.

Furthermore, based on the 'Open Heart' study, Barbara concluded that when participants cultivated these open-hearted moments through mindfulness meditation, they elevated their daily intake of positivity. In this study, participants were randomised into two groups, with one group was subjected to daily doses of positivity through mindfulness meditation, while the other group didn't receive any intervention. After three months, they found that the participants who received the intervention became more mindful and aware of their surroundings. They got better at savouring what was good in their lives and found more solutions to problems. These effects were not just temporary but created enduring mental habits. Thus, mindfulness has similar effects to positive emotions based on this research. Barbara also concluded that positivity and mindfulness feed on each other, each triggering and reinforcing the other. This bidirectional link signifies that another lever you can grasp to increase positivity is to be open and mindful. Barbara's research concluded that mindfulness training teaches people to do something that comes automatically with positive emotions. It teaches people to open their minds. Openness and positivity are attached, causing, and amplifying each other. The newly cultivated openness throws open the door to positivity, creating an upward spiral of well-being.

Emotional Awareness

Over the last two decades, especially after Daniel Goleman's book *Emotional Intelligence*, a lot of importance is being given to emotional awareness in both personal and professional spheres. In fact, many HR professionals prioritise Emotional Quotient (EQ) over Intelligence Quotient (IQ). This makes a lot of sense because whether employees are in leadership roles or not, they are required to work as a team. The more aware and mindful we are of our emotions, the more empathetic and compassionate we can be towards others.

Health And Disease

Stress and health are closely related, multiple studies show how stress and anxiety correlate with illness and disease. As a gastroenterologist, I have seen in my practice of over two decades how gastrointestinal diseases like Irritable Bowel Syndrome (IBS), dyspepsia, and others are often associated with increasing anxiety, stress, and fear. We have also recently seen an increased occurrence of heart attacks in India, especially among younger people, where stress has played an important role.

Thus, introducing mindfulness as a practice to alleviate stress and anxiety is advisable, and many doctors and hospitals are using it widely. The MBSR (Mindfulness-Based Stress Reduction) programme, developed by Dr Jon Kabat-Zinn, includes an eight-week structured programme of mindfulness, and it has been widely used across the globe with profound benefits. It has been found to cause a significant reduction in blood pressure, diabetes, headache, anxiety, and chronic fatigue, among other illnesses.

Creativity

More and more research is showing that mindfulness can have a favourable impact on creativity. We may know from our own experience that we are most creative when we are open, curious, and present, and a relaxed state, such as when showering, meditating, or walking, can augment many brilliant ideas. Mindfulness has been found to be a wonderful tool for enhancing creativity as well. The open monitoring meditation techniques—in which there is no specific focus of awareness—are effective in promoting divergent thinking—the ability to find many different solutions to problems, which is strongly correlated with creativity.

Sports

Every sportsperson or athlete will wholeheartedly agree that in sports, the mental component plays a huge role. When a cricketer faces a routine slump in form, it is mostly the mind playing tricks on them, making their footwork and drives more tentative and increasing the risk of getting out.

Mindfulness has been used in the training of various sports events because it is widely recognised that only when the player is alert, present, and focused, can he or she perform best. If a footballer is going for a crucial penalty shoot and worries about the chances of scoring a goal, it will definitely affect his performance. But if they were to totally focus on the present moment and only target the goal and goalkeeper, their entire outlook will be different.

Psychologists Dr Keith Kauffman, Dr Timothy Pineau, and Dr Carol Glass wrote the book *Mindful Sports Performance Enhancement*, where they elaborate on these techniques. The more present and mindful the athletes are, the more likely they are to be in the zone, which is a harbinger of peak performances. When they are aware of the thoughts, sensations, and anxieties they are facing within, it creates a space for their feelings to unfold and prevents them from becoming overwhelmed.

During his remarkable career with the Chicago Bulls and Los Angeles Lakers, Phil Jackson won more championships than any coach in the history of professional sports. He led his teams to the NBA Championship eleven times—six times with Chicago Bulls and five times with the Los Angeles Lakers). Jackson attributes much of his coaching success to the implementation of mindfulness and Zen Buddhism, inspiring legends like Michael Jordan, Shaquille O' Neal, and Kobe Bryant to astounding success. His book, *Eleven Rings*, co-authored with Hugh Delehanty, chronicles this incredible journey of success, leadership, and mindfulness.

Practising Mindfulness

Now that we have covered the 'why' aspect in some detail, let's address the most important part of it all: the 'how?' How do we go about practicing mindfulness? There are so many myths associated with mindfulness and meditation that these often come in the way of those who wish to start the practice. That's why I deliberately use the word 'practice'.

It is more direct and practical to refer to it the practice of returning to the present moment. It is universal and entirely secular, which is a significant reason for its popularity. There are no rituals, dogmas, or religious beliefs attached to it. It transcends all religions and beliefs because it focuses on the present moment, which doesn't belong to any particular religion or creed.

Usually, when we practice, we use an anchor that grounds us in the present moment. The most used anchor is the breath, but we can use any sensory stimulation, such as sounds, vision, taste, smell, or touch, to anchor us because our senses are all in the present moment. We don't hear or see in the past or future. We can even forgo any anchor and simply remain aware of whatever is occurring in our experience.

Mindfulness With the Breath

The process is simple. Choose a comfortable place to sit, whether a chair, sofa, or cushion. You can also practice lying down, but be cautious as you may fall asleep. You don't need to adopt any specific sitting posture; just sit comfortably, as you would in your office chair or at home. If you are using a cushion, assume a comfortable cross-legged position.

Now take a moment to identify where you can easily feel your breath. It may be through the breath entering your nostrils, the movement of your chest, or the rise and fall of your abdomen. Focus on your normal, everyday breathing, not deep or forced breaths. Simply become aware of your breath as you inhale and exhale and follow it gently.

When you are seated in a comfortable position and following your breath, you may encounter a common challenge—your thoughts. There is a widespread misconception that you need to stop your thoughts completely, or else the practice is futile. This is not the case. Simply allow your thoughts to be as they are, without engaging in them or suppressing them. Zen master Shunryū Suzuki put it eloquently: 'Leave your front door and your back door open. Let thoughts come and go. Just don't serve them tea.'

Many people, when starting mindfulness or meditation practice, struggle with their thoughts, attempting to suppress them. I, too, faced this difficulty, and often became frustrated and exhausted. The more I suppressed them, the stronger these thoughts became. It was only when I let them come and go without giving them any extra attention could I sit for longer periods. The trick is to simply accept and allow them, rather than chasing them away. The moment you get entangled in your thoughts, gently return to the anchor, your breath. Label the thoughts as 'thinking' and return to the present moment. Every time you come back to the present moment, you are breaking the cycle of being absent or unmindful. Thoughts, feelings, and everything else within your awareness are all part of the practice.

Mindfulness with Sounds

We are always surrounded by sounds, whether it's traffic sounds while travelling or the sounds in our workplace and homes. For many people, sounds maybe be a deterrent to any mindful activity, and one of the biggest misconceptions is that perfect silence is required for any mindfulness practice. Therefore, it must be limited to our home, often in a secluded corner. This discourages many as they find it challenging, burdensome, and impractical.

Sounds can be a wonderful anchor to bring us into the present moment. Just like the breath, sounds or any sensory experience can serve as a portal to the present moment. The key is not to engage with or suppress thoughts, but simply to be aware of the sounds. When you bring your awareness to sounds, it's not about their content or volume, but the sensation of sound.

The practice is quite simple. Sit comfortably in any suitable position and bring your awareness to the sounds around you.

You can keep your eyes open or closed, though closing them initially can help you keep away from distractions. Whenever you get distracted by your thoughts, remember to neither engage nor suppress them. Simply return to the sounds. It doesn't matter what sounds you hear, do not label or judge them.

Another useful practice is to occasionally alternate between the breath and the sounds. I find switching from one anchor to another quite useful, especially when tired or easily distracted.

Thus, you can be creative with your mindfulness approach. I often use mindfulness with sounds as a useful anchor when I'm travelling to work in the morning. I am blessed to have a driver, and as I sit in the back, I use all the background sounds, which blend into a single seamless sound, as an anchor for stillness. By the time I reach the hospital, I am calm and relaxed. I practice the same at airports after checking-in as it can be a pleasant experience to fuse all the background sounds—chatting and people's movement—into a single humming sound. Bringing awareness to all these sounds is a productive way to pass the time while awaiting the departure of your flight. You can also use taste, smell, sights, and open awareness of all sensations as anchors.

Mindfulness on the Go

Jon Kabat-Zinn says, 'The real meditation is how we lead our lives.' The art of mindfulness is using it throughout the day, from waking up until sleeping, to enhance the quality of our life and relationships.

When we wake up in the morning and brush our teeth and wash our face, we can mentally label the act as brushing or washing. We may not be fully present upon waking up, but by labelling it, we ensure we are not going through the process on autopilot mode. Taking a bath with awareness can be a refreshing and soothing way to enter the present moment, experiencing the touch of water on our bodies, the scent of soap, all can be enjoyed with presence. Then, when we are getting ready, we can mentally label it as putting on a shirt or belt.

Often, I am in a hurry in the morning, as most of us are, but being present need not mean slowing down. We can be quick in awareness. Even being mindful of just putting on a shirt or belt can break us out of the cycle of mindlessness. When we enter our car or whatever mode of transport we use, we can simply mentally say 'opening the door' or 'sitting down'. Such a small gesture goes a long way into becoming more mindful. It may seem like a minor adjustment, but these can soon start rewiring our nervous system so that the more we do it, the more it gets reinforced.

Meena Srinivasan, author and mindfulness expert, outlines the 4Ts (tea, toilet, telephone, transition) that we can comfortably use in our workplace, even if we are working at home.

Tea or coffee breaks are ubiquitous and allow us a moment to come back to the present. Instead of mindlessly sipping tea or snacking, we can consciously bring our awareness to these activities:

a) We often use the toilet or washroom, particularly to wash our hands. As a doctor, I wash my hands between every patient, giving me a chance to be present again. Feeling the sensation of water and soap in our hands can instinctively make us mindful once more.

b) Our mobile phones are on incessantly throughout the day and it gives us another opportunity to become present again. If not every time, once in a while, when we see messages or notifications or answer the phone, we can use that time to bring us back into the present.

c) We are always in transition between one activity and another and yet again it provides us an opportunity to break the cycle of mindlessness. In my case, when I move from the outpatient department to the endoscopy room or when going for rounds, I deliberately walk mindfully, becoming aware of my movements and actions, enabling me to return to the present moment.

d) Those working at home are also always in transition from one task to another, or from one room to another. These are all opportunities to become mindful again and break the cycle of mindlessness.

Mindful Eating

Mindful eating is a wonderful way to incorporate mindfulness practice into your daily life and greatly enhance the joy of eating. Most times, we eat our meals mindlessly on the go, checking our phones or watching the TV. This often leads to overeating because satiety signals from the stomach reach the brain after a lag period of a few minutes. If we eat in a hurry, the brain does not register it. Also, since we are in such a rush, we hardly ever savour our meals and are unaware of what we have eaten.

Mindful eating is about being aware of the process of eating right from the moment the food enters our mouth. Take a minute to reflect with gratitude on how this food item has reached your plate from some far-off place and due to the efforts of farmers, and how we are all interconnected and interdependent.

Before eating, check how hungry you really are and what your body signs tell you. Notice the shape, colour, texture, and aroma of the food in front of you. Allow the food to be in your mouth, let it mix with saliva, and mindfully chew. Slowly and deliberately chew your food before swallowing it—stay aware of the urge to swallow it, instead of mindlessly gulping it. After swallowing, follow the meal to the stomach, taste the flavour of the food, and start the process of putting food in your mouth again.

You may not be able to do this with every meal, but even if you follow this process once a day, you bring awareness, joy, and taste to your mealtime while adding mindfulness to one of the basic activities. In fact, when pressed for time, even being mindful for a few bites can bring one back to the present. When we eat mindfully, we enjoy the crunch of an apple, the sweet chill of an ice-cream, or even the quenching effect of water when we are thirsty. Try drinking a glass of water when really thirsty and savour the first few sips. It is sheer ambrosia.

Mindful Communication

Communication is an integral part of our professional and personal lives. Most times, we are so lost in our thoughts and worries that we are hardly present for the other person. When we are listening, we are already preparing our answer and, as a result, cannot connect at a deeper level. Mindful communication is about deep empathetic listening and attention. In fact, mindfulness is a process through which we learn to listen to ourselves, our thoughts, and our emotions. It may seem paradoxical, but mindful communication begins with oneself, and then extends to the other.

Janice Marturano, author of *Finding the Space to Lead: A Practical Guide to Mindful Leadership* and founder of the Institute for Mindful Leadership, describes a process of mindful communication based on Gregory Kramer's methodology (author of *Insight Dialogue*). It involves a four-step process that can be broken down into simple steps but seamlessly woven into one smooth process.

1. Pause, because when you do so, you have an opportunity to check in with yourself and your feelings. You can use the sensations of your breath or feel your body to become present so that you can enter the communication with your whole being—mind, body, and spirit.

2. Open up to what is here rather than what you may have imagined, expected, or hoped for. Rather than taking your bias and expectations into the communication, which prevent you from being fully here, be willing to go in with an open mind.

3. Listen deeply and redirect your focus when you notice the quality of your attention waning. It also includes listening to yourself, to the sensations and thoughts that arise within when others are speaking.

4. Speak the truth with the intention to do no harm. It requires a culture that makes it safe for each person to speak their truth.

David Rome, founder of 'Mindful Focusing', describes deep listening as learning to listen from a deeper place in oneself to a deeper place in others. Centred in our own grounded aware presence, we are able to extend friendly attention to others. The primary catalyst, according to him, is not asking questions or giving answers, but the palpable quality of our listening. Our simple human presence, offered with no agenda, provides a safe and empowering space for others to go deep into themselves and invite fresh knowing to emerge.

Hearing vs Listening

Evelyn Glenie, a famous Scottish percussionist, became deaf at the early age of twelve. This did not prevent her from pursuing a career in music. She was selected as one of the two laureates for the Polar Music Prize. In an interview, she discussed the difference between hearing and listening. She said that she couldn't hear due to her deafness, but that never prevented her from listening. She poignantly shared what listening meant to her: 'Listening is an action that we decide to engage with. My body is a huge ear, therefore my legs, scalp, fingertips, feet and much more all engage in the listening process. Listening is about opening up the channels of our physical body rather than overloading our ears. Listening is about observing what we see, smell, touch and taste just as the acoustics of a concert hall is my instrument that I paint sound to. The instrument I play is simply a tool. I don't hear an acoustic when I stand still in the hall but I feel its weight and presence. What is the weight of your listening?'

According to her, deep listening is not about class, structure, age, race, colour or anything else, but about tapping into what is inside of us and what we tell ourselves.

Mindful Walking

Mindful walking offers us the chance to bring our practice out of the cushion into our everyday lives. We are always in motion, travelling from one place to the other. But often in our haste to reach a certain destination, we miss the aliveness of life right now. We forget that while we are walking, we are alive, and it is a blessing to be able to use all our limbs effectively.

When we walk mindfully, every step becomes a gift. We feel the movement of our feet and hands, the contact of the feet on the ground, the sensation of the skin on our face, and this automatically breaks the cycle of mindlessness, transporting us into the present. We can either dedicate a few formal mindful minutes to walking every day, or whenever we remember, we can simply be aware of our movements and return to the body, which is always in the present moment.

Being Open to this Moment

Our most important realisation is that our willingness to get up close and intimate with this moment is the portal to freedom and happiness. The author and teacher Amoda Maa beautifully wrote in her book *Embodied Enlightenment*, 'The mind-shattering magnificence of existence can only be truly available to you in the willingness to be open to intimacy and all that appears in each moment.' This moment is always here, she says, it never leaves you or abandons you. Take a moment to rest here and allow yourself to be open to all that is. We simply have to remain open to the fear, resistance, the vulnerability, and the beauty of this moment as it is.

Mindfulness is the path of the sacred middle, neither desperately going back to the past nor apprehensively fearing the future but being present with whatever is right here, at this very moment.

Practices

- Take pauses from time to time through the day. When you are travelling in the car or while walking, pause to take in the breeze or feel the sun on your face. When you are in the office in between activities, you can pause for a few seconds and simply be aware of what you are doing.

- Make a habit of checking in with your body. What are you feeling now? Can you feel a tightness or openness? Just stay with it without trying to change it.

- Practise asking yourself from time to time: Am I present? Then, come back to the present moment.

- When you are sitting down, take a few seconds to acknowledge that you are sitting. Just feel your back against the chair and feet against the ground.

- When you are waiting for someone, just be conscious of your breath. Stay present with whatever is going on within you, instead of aimlessly scrolling on the phone.

- Be aware of all sounds in your vicinity. Sit and close your eyes. Allow yourself to be aware of all the sounds, voices, and sensations.

- Practise mindful communication by listening to others. Take a partner and give complete attention for three minutes without interrupting them. Then take turns and switch roles. Do not seek any advice or feedback, just friendly presence while each explores the topic and the feeling it brings with them.

- Rather than mindlessly sipping tea, bring yourself back to the present moment. Sip the tea in awareness, savour the sweet, warm brew and feel the warmth of the cup.

- Sit wherever you are and sense the aliveness in your body. Can you feel the tingling in your hands or feet, or just the sensation of being alive?

- When you enter the car, pause before starting the engine, and breathe consciously. Take a few seconds to feel the steering wheel, the gear, and be mindful of your back against the seat and feet on the ground.

- Perform any small task by being present and mindful and observe how you feel from within. Hold a cup, drink water, or write a few words while being in the present and see if you can feel a sense of expansiveness within.

4

NAVIGATING FEAR, CULTIVATING COURAGE, AND EMBRACING VULNERABILITY

'Fear is the cheapest room in the house.
I would like to see you living in better conditions.'

—Hafiz

This book would be incomplete without my dedicating a chapter to fear because it marked the beginning of the most significant transformation of my life, which I have previously referred to as being twice born. The way we handle fear significantly influences our lives. Do we push it away, avoid it, or are we willing to confront it?

For most of my life, my relationship with fear was like anyone else's. Mostly, I tried to fix, modify, and soften it wherever possible. This continued until I reached a point where all escape routes were closed. Life had truly cornered me, leaving me alone with the overwhelming, claustrophobic sensation of fear. Pema Chödrön discusses this in her book *When Things Fall Apart*, asking, 'What do you do when you meet your edge; how to become intimate with fear when there is no escape?'

After Rashmi developed the life-threatening complication and went for surgery, intense fear consumed me for days.

My instinct was to sit with this feeling and become intimate with it since there was no alternative. The only way was to go through it. With a background in meditation and mindfulness, I did just that, sitting with apprehension and dread as much as possible. Initially, it seemed dark and terrifying, and my first reaction was that it would overwhelm me, and I wouldn't be able to survive it. Still, I took small steps, attempting to stay with it for short periods and to identify its location in the body by staying fully present with it. Simply acknowledging it, noting the tight constriction in my chest, the sense of impending doom in the heart, or the sinking feeling in the abdomen, created a gap between the emotion and myself.

The longer I stayed with the feeling and the discomfort, the more I noticed a subtle shift. The fear remained, but a slight space began to emerge around it. A small opening had been created around it which was like a crack. The more I acknowledged and allowed the feeling, the wider the space grew, gradually embracing the emotion. Now, it wasn't just fear; it was fear and a warm presence comforting it.

Pema Chödrön teaches that we must delve into the heart of the emotion to transcend it. Fear is like a dot in front of us, a doorway we could go through, but destination is uncertain. Since we try to protect ourselves from what will hurt us, we avoid going inward, escalating the fear. Resistance to fear amplifies the issue. When we acknowledge and stay with fear, becoming fully present with it, we can then enter the state of presence and fearlessness.

Fear is a universal experience and part of our existence, serving an evolutionary role to protect us. However, over time, we have lost the ability to connect with it and freeze at the first sign. Pema encourages us to explore whether we can be present with the fear without our narratives, to embrace it and lean into it instead of backing off or acting out.

Our instinct is to repress fear because it is uncomfortable to sit with shakiness, a racing heart, or a queasy stomach. Pema suggests that it is the warrior's path to learn to perk up and lean in rather than collapse and back away. As Psychologist Susan David puts it, 'Courage is not the absence of fear but fear walking.'

This state of groundlessness is tender and pulsating, and when we stay with it, courage and compassion begin to take root. When we turn towards fear, touch its rawness, and keep our hearts open, we are blessed with immense wisdom. This state is beautifully described in the poem 'When You Stop Running Away' by Jeff Foster:

If you sit
just long enough
with sadness, fear or longing
or some strange energy
or urge you can't even name
if you sit in a place of no hope and no expectation
if you open your heart wide in meditation
the sadness eventually softens
the fear becomes intimate
its imagined edges and boundaries dissolving into the
vastness
and it reveals its deep intelligence and benevolent
nature
for at the core of everything we run away from
is everything we long for
but we'll never know
if we keep running.

I had encountered intense fear before. I remember a time years ago when there was turmoil in my family, and my father had a massive heart attack. On the day he was to be discharged from the hospital, a heated argument erupted among family members. I was terrified about how my father would react, and I couldn't sleep all night, dreading the outcome when he came home.

That was intense, terrifying fear, but during such instances and while dealing with fear, I would pray and hope for the best and bear the ordeal through gritted teeth, pushing the feeling away. However, this crisis made me realise that only a radical shift could help me. That shift involved moving into the heart of fear and investigating its source and origin.

Where does it arise? What is its source? Moving into fear goes against our usual instincts. In the upcoming chapter on emotions, I mention that we often view fear and our dark emotions as dense and permanent. We believe they stick with us once they visit. However, mindfulness practice reveals that our emotions have a limited life. They are made of energy enveloped in our awareness. When we sit in awareness, we notice that behind our strongest emotions, there is the light of presence and awareness. This realisation is transformative and forms the basis of emotional alchemy.

Tara Brach, psychologist, author, and spiritual teacher, identifies two major fears that humans face daily: The fear of failure (FOF) and the fear of missing out (FOMO). FOF arises from the primitive (reptilian) part of our brain, which believes it is separate and isolated, and constantly fears rejection.

FOMO, on the other hand, is a more mammalian response, arising from the fear of missing out on pleasures and opportunities. Brach advises us to notice our thoughts regarding our separate self and directly connect with our emotions.

In my case, while dealing with fear, I realised that more than the fear itself, what terrified me more were the thoughts and stories my mind created about being a failure and letting people down. I would hear unpleasant recurring thoughts like: 'What would my colleagues think of me?' This particular patient had waited for my return from an international conference, and the whole family had placed their trust in me. I could hear a voice chastising me, thinking I should have done things differently, even though deep down, I knew that nothing would have changed the outcome.

The only way to prevent these destructive thoughts from overwhelming us is to sit with the feelings. By being open to our fear, we prevent thoughts from assaulting us. We connect fully with the physical sensations instead of being drowned in thoughts. While thoughts may cause distress, the shift occurs when we focus on the emotion without letting the thoughts in. This disrupts the thought-emotion cycle.

We need to realise that these stories are fictions sustained by our feelings and emotions. What our fear needs most is courage and loving acceptance. When we lean into the emotions and connect with the direct experience of the feeling, the stories gradually fall apart. This is why leaning into fear with presence and mindfulness can be so transformative.

Resisting fear exacerbates it. When fear manifests in our bodies as contractions, constrictions, or heaviness, we often resist and numb ourselves through distraction or busyness. This resistance intensifies the response. The courageous approach is to lean into fear and face it, as the saying goes, 'Feel it to Heal it.' Otherwise, we may spend our entire lives running away from our fears. As Pema Chödrön eloquently states, 'Nothing ever goes away until it has taught us what we need to know'. This was a profound lesson for me. If I didn't have the courage to befriend my fear and learn from it, it would haunt me indefinitely.

John J. Prendergast, psychologist and author of *The Deep Heart: Our Portal to Presence*, talks about allowing the space of presence to hold our fears in its embrace. When we allow ourselves to lean into our fears, it can act as an important portal to fearlessness and presence. This presence may be experienced as a kind of stillness in the midst of turbulence and is a reflection of our inner nature.

Learning to sit with even intense feelings and pain reveals that they can be held within a larger, open space that is still and non-judgmental, accommodating even the most intense emotions. This presence is our true nature, indestructible, whole, and compassionate.

Courageous Presence

When discussing fear, how can we not talk about fearlessness and courage? Facing our fears and being willing to stay with our terror, helplessness, and sadness requires tremendous bravery. It is not a process for the faint-hearted. It is a process of opening to the unknown, not shying from uncomfortable feelings, nor giving up on ourselves. Tara Brach describes this process of opening up to our fears as courageous presence and describes the three steps that facilitate it.

The first is to notice what is happening, to be aware of all the myriad disturbing feelings and emotions within our body and acknowledge their presence. The next step is to feel and connect with them, leaning into and embracing the raw, tender feelings and sensations without trying to push them away. Willingness to open to these raw feelings allows a wider presence to hold us in its warm embrace.

The final step is to respond with wisdom and non-judgement. Rather than reacting and lashing out, we can create space around our feelings and respond to the situation with gentleness and openness. Chögyam Rinpoche, a prominent teacher of Tibetan Buddhism, describes fearlessness as the ability to examine fear closely. Only then can we transcend it. The path to bravery is the quiet power of standing by yourself, within yourself, in the depths of your own heart. It is being present with your entire experience without the need to alter or modify it. Spiritual writer and philosopher Mark Nepo poignantly describes this as 'exquisite risk'. In his book, *Inner Courage*, Nepo distinguishes between outer and inner courage. Outer courage, which we all admire, involves finding unexpected strength to face dangerous situations, like plunging into a river to save a drowning child. However, it grows from another kind of courage, which is inner courage. He defines inner courage as the foundation of quiet braveries from which the more visible ones sprout. This constitutes courage in its deepest sense, made up of courage to feel, to see, to accept, to heal, and to be. When we feel terrified and helpless, on the verge of breaking down but are still willing to stand and show up for ourselves, it is the height of fearlessness. Our relationship with fear and fearlessness, hopelessness and bravery, sets the tone for our relationship with life.

Nepo advocates summoning the courage to face the river at the bottom of our ravines of fear, loss, and broken openness, and in the process discovering a glimpse of our eternal reality. Faced with harrowing losses or overwhelming fears, it may be difficult to believe that anything of value can be found in such painful experiences, but here is where we need tremendous patience and courage to let the universe reveal its treasures.

I can only speak of my own experiences of facing my demons of fear and despair and am grateful for the strength and courage the universe bestowed upon me to be open to my inner experiences and venture into scary places. Sometimes it is grace that makes you confront a situation when you are well and truly cornered and have no place to hide. That journey into my deepest fears revealed an entire world within me which was unexplored and may have still been untouched if it were not for this experience in my life. I am inspired and find a lot of truth in these words of Elisabeth Kübler-Ross, 'Should you shield the canyons from the windstorms you would never see the true beauty of their carvings.'

Courage to Face Death

Among all the fears that we face, none is as intense as the fear of facing death. It requires immense courage to confront death head-on. No one describes this more beautifully than Frank Ostaseski, a Buddhist teacher who ran a Zen hospice for the dying many years ago. He penned down his reflections in his extraordinary book, *Five Invitations: Discovering What Death Can Teach Us About Living Fully*, after witnessing death and dying up close.

More than being about death, the book is an invitation and guide to making the most of life. It invites us to live and love each moment so fully that, at the time of death, there are no regrets at not having savoured life enough. Frank eloquently writes that death is not something waiting for us at the end of a long road; it is always with us, in the marrow of each passing moment. As a teacher and guide, death shows us what is most important to make each moment count.

According to Frank, his book is an invitation to sit down with death and have a cup of tea with her. We may ask why we would to do that. Well, if we want to live a rich and meaningful life, fully intimate with each moment, there is no better teacher than death. He observed that many of his patients increasingly discovered profound truths about love, life, and meaning as they approached their final moments. But we don't need to wait until we are about to die to discover these profound gems. His five invitations are simple yet profound, always present but often ignored due to mundane preoccupations:

1. Don't wait: Avoid postponing happiness indefinitely, as many dying individuals regret.
2. Welcome everything, push away nothing: Embrace every experience, even the challenging and painful ones, for they hold valuable lessons.

3. Bring your whole self to the experience: Be authentic and don't hide aspects of your personality or experiences, as your own suffering, vulnerability, and helplessness can benefit others.

4. Find a place of rest in the middle of things: Regardless of external circumstances, you can find inner peace.

5. Cultivate a don't know mind: Maintain a beginner's mind and let life continue to delight and amaze you. To quote Shunryu Suzuki from his book, *Zen Mind, Beginner's Mind*, 'In the beginner's mind there are many possibilities, but in the expert's there are few.'

These five invitations help us keep death close at hand and teach us to delight in each moment. We learn to celebrate life by welcoming it with an open mind and open heart, humility, and fearlessness.

Vulnerability

Vulnerability is a close relative of fear and courage. We fear our vulnerability and will go to great lengths to protect it. However, true courage lies in embracing our vulnerability fully. In the words of Brené Brown, the renowned researcher on vulnerability, 'Vulnerability is our most accurate way to measure courage, and we can measure how brave we are by how vulnerable we are willing to be.'

Contrary to what we have been brought up to believe, vulnerability is not a sign of weakness. According to Brown, it is 'the birthplace of intimacy, true connection, creativity, and joy. It sounds like truth and feels like courage.' Truth and courage aren't always comfortable, but they are never our weaknesses. It's the point where fear and courage intersect.

In my journey of confronting fear, I became well-acquainted with my vulnerability. Like many others, I considered vulnerability to be a sign of weakness and did my best to wear an armour to shield myself. Until this tragedy occurred and exposed my deepest fear, bringing it out into the open.

My greatest fear was of being shamed, ridiculed, and humiliated, and in this case, all these feelings surged to the surface. However, in my efforts to save my patient's life, I was willing to expose myself to all the shame and humiliation that could come my way. I discussed the case openly with many colleagues and seniors and advised the family to seek as many medical opinions as needed. I was willing to expose myself and my failure openly, as long as it would help my patient somehow. I would pick up the phone and dial my colleagues or friends and frankly tell them how helpless I felt and inquire if any other measures could be taken to save the patient. It was both to discuss the treatment aspect as well as allow my feelings to flow.

Unfortunately, none of this could save her, but it taught me a valuable lesson. A lesson in embracing my own fear, shame, and vulnerability. The greatest blessing of embracing vulnerability was, having touched my deepest fear, it opened the doorway to exquisite joy. My heart seemed to have magically opened.

Brené Brown eloquently says, 'Vulnerability is not winning or losing; it's having the courage to show up and be seen when we have no control over the outcome.' This is something I wholeheartedly agree with as there are times when we feel helpless. However, just showing up during such moments of despair is a sign of immense courage.

We also need to understand that we try to shield ourselves from our vulnerability and protect our fragile ego because we fear being overwhelmed. But in our journey of discovering our true nature, we discover that we are much larger than our fragile ego, and we don't need to protect what is at our core. We must also remember that when we try to selectively protect ourselves from dark feelings, we also numb ourselves to positive ones. So, when we numb our fear, shame, and vulnerability, we also numb joy, gratitude, and happiness.

Writing this book, especially the chapters on my encounters with fear, shame, humiliation, and despair, has been a significant lesson for me in vulnerability and courage. To be so open and honest about one's feelings is akin to standing naked in the middle of a marketplace with hundreds of people looking at you—exposed, raw, and open to ridicule and judgement. This is even more challenging when you are still active in the medical profession and risk being judged and ridiculed. However, I was determined to write in as much detail and depth as possible because I know that reading about my journey will be a source of healing and wisdom for many others. To quote feminist and civil rights activist, Audre Lorde in her essay, 'The Transformation of Silence into Language and Action, 'I have come to believe over and over again that what is most important to me must be spoken, made verbal and shared, even at the risk of having it bruised or misunderstood'.

We all go through various experiences and trials and tribulations in life, and each one has unique lessons to offer. We can learn from each other's experiences and become wiser, rather than letting our pain and suffering be in vain. As author Robin MacArthur says, 'Revealing oneself is an act of radical generosity, letting oneself be seen allows others to do the same. And this vulnerability creates connection; this connection creates community.'

I never really wanted to face fear so closely, but I now know that it has been one of the biggest gifts of my life. When your heart is ripped open, and you are barely able to breathe, and the very core of your being is permeated by intense emotions, can you still face it? I realised that fear and pain are the gateway to fearlessness. You are allowed entry to this gate when you fully accept and surrender to the feeling without resisting or pushing it away. What you encounter is a taste of your own indestructibility.

Subsequently, there have been several encounters with fear, and they have never failed to teach me something significant each time. During the last couple of years fear has turned our whole life around with the dreaded pandemic. When my wife and daughter contracted Covid during the first wave, and I caught it in the deadly second wave, my family and I suffered intense fear and terror as people were dying around us. The fear of illness, losing our loved ones, or fear for our own life can be extremely intense to experience. This also provided another opportunity to sit with fear, bring it closer and explore it.

I can't say that the fear was any less intense. But when I stripped the stories from the feeling, I became aware that the smell and taste of the fear was the same. It can be fear of any reason of any kind, but the process involved in entering into fearlessness remains the same. Bring it close, lean into it, accept it fully without resisting it in any way. This is a lifelong process indeed, but my invitation to all the readers is that the next time fear comes close to you, don't push it away. Don't avoid it or distract yourself. See if you can be brave enough to approach it, and you will be in for a big surprise. A surprise that may well change your life.

Practices

- Notice when fear arises within you. Can you observe it? Can you simply label it as fear? Labelling and naming it create space around it.
- Choose either a real-life or imaginary situation where intense fear surrounds you. Try to locate this

feeling within your body, whether it's a heaviness in the chest or a sinking sensation in the belly. Stay with it for a few seconds.

- Once you get comfortable with staying, imagine the same situation and see if you can sit with the feeling for a longer period.

- Respond to a situation after staying with fear. Allow the fear to remain within your body. Feel it, and then respond instead of merely reacting.

- Identify what makes you feel most vulnerable. List situations, such as openly sharing your emotions or public speaking. Reflect on why you feel vulnerable in certain situations or with specific people. What thoughts are circulating in your mind? Is it the fear of exposure, the fear of being ridiculed, or the fear of revealing your emotions?

- Can you sit with a feeling of anxiety or dread for a brief period? Try to feel the anxiety within your body.

- How do you cope with your vulnerability? Do you transform this feeling into expressions of anger, irritation, or tears?

- Notice how when fear arises, you tend to immediately depart from your body and escape into your mind, thinking fearful thoughts and imagining dreadful scenarios. Can you return to the present moment, to the immediacy of your body—just breathe, sit, and be present?

- Can you think of a situation in which you can bring your whole self? Reflect on how you can show compassion and empathy to someone because you have experienced something quite similar in your life.

- For a few moments, can you find the courage to contemplate your mortality? Can you confront the thought of dying? It's not a morbid thought but can help you cherish every moment as more precious.

5

EMOTIONAL MINDFULNESS AND ALCHEMY

'Our greatest gifts and deepest wounds reside in the same area.'
—Michael Meade

'How are you feeling?' I asked my friend. He looked surprised, and replied with a perfunctory, 'Fine, cool. How about you?' I interrupted him to clarify that I was asking about his emotional state, not his general well-being. This time he was taken aback, but used to my quirky ways, he decided to humour me, 'Don't they mean the same? Anyway, let me see,' he pondered, pausing. 'I'm feeling a little restless and distracted, but come to think of it, I wouldn't have realised it or given it any importance to it if you hadn't inquired.'

This is what most of us do. We are rarely aware of our current emotional state, either because we don't see its purpose, or, more likely, because we might fear delving into the unknown. Who knows what we may encounter? When we catch even a whiff of discomforting feelings surfacing, we usually smother them, push them aside, or override them with more pleasant feelings.

What transpires when we pause during the day and ask ourselves, 'How am I feeling?' It offers an insight into our mental state, and very often, that brief pause prevents us from impulsively acting on our emotions. Upon introspection, we may experience restlessness, apprehension, joy, or sadness. There's no need to judge, modify, or create a narrative around it. It just is. However, that pause creates a small space around the emotion, which gives us the choice to respond with balance. More importantly, it opens a portal within us. This is the essence of emotional mindfulness.

For a significant part of my life, I was somewhat emotionally illiterate. I have been fortunate to possess a cheerful disposition and generally good nature. But whenever I felt the stirrings of uncomfortable or negative emotions, I would assume I had done something wrong and promptly push them aside or distract myself with an activity.

This is what I observed others doing while growing up, and it appeared to be a safe approach. I was under the impression that the presence of uncomfortable emotions meant that there was something awry, and it was safest to suppress them there and then.

Skilful and Unskilful Emotions

It was only through my mindfulness practice that I realised my emotional illiteracy and the common tendency to numb our feelings, remaining disconnected from what lies beneath the surface. Dzogchen Ponlop Rinpoche, Buddhist teacher and author of *Emotional Rescue*, explains that we often mistakenly label emotions as positive or negative. A wiser approach is to describe them as skilful or unskilful. Emotions represent a blend of energy and thoughts that infuse our lives with vibrancy and colour. Ponlop asserts that a life without emotions is inconceivable, akin to having soda without fizz. What we must grasp is how to handle our emotions with greater skill and mindfulness.

In his book *Emotional Intimacy*, Robert Augustus Masters asserts the essential nature of emotional intimacy for truly fulfilling and vibrant relationships. He describes emotional intimacy as: a) becoming intimate with our emotions, including their origin, expression, historical roots, and relational impact; and b) becoming intimate in our relationships with significant others through how we express and share our emotions. This level of intimacy allows us to make the best use of all our emotions including the so-called dark or shadow emotions. Masters suggests that modelling a healthy relationship with our emotions is one of the biggest gifts we can offer our children.

Many of us have experienced the consequences of our parents' unresolved emotional wounds. My father, a compassionate and noble soul, occasionally displayed temper and anger outbursts that left us quite scared and shaken. Relatives informed me that anger was a prevalent issue in our family tree, and we simply had to simply endure it. This spurred a determination not to inherit this unskilful trait and sparked a subconsciously interest in understanding our emotions and how to manage them.

Emotional Mindfulness

As defined earlier, mindfulness is about being aware of the present moment—both within and without—the way it is, non-judgementally. When we develop the ability to stay in the present moment using our breath or any of our senses as an anchor, we begin to become aware of our emotions, feelings, and thoughts. Mindfulness isn't about suppressing or getting rid of emotions to attain equanimity; it's about engaging with our emotions more skilfully.

Most emotions are a blend of physical, mental, and affective experiences. For instance, when we become angry, physical changes like muscle tension and a sensation of heat occur, along with a conceptual storyline explaining the anger.

There's also a felt sense component, which we may often overlook.

When we sit in awareness, various thoughts and emotions flood our mind. They may be vague emotions like restlessness, agitation, or stronger ones like fear or sadness. The first step is to observe and acknowledge these emotions. This is a departure from our normal practice of distancing ourselves from uncomfortable emotions. Acknowledging emotions allows them to be as they are, sans judgement. The next step, then, is to label the emotions, such as fear, anxiety, or sadness.

The second step is to name the emotions. Dr Daniel Siegel, a clinical professor of psychiatry at the UCLA School of Medicine and executive director of the Mindsight Institute, recommends an exercise called 'affect labelling'. This process allows us 'name it to tame it'. This simple act of labelling our strong emotions reduces activity in the brain's emotional centres, including the amygdala, empowering the frontal lobes. By naming our emotions we can observe them, implying that the emotion is separate from us.

When we pause to ask ourselves what we feel and give it a name, we create a much-needed space when reactive emotions are rising. Naming and acknowledging our feelings help us create a distance and observe them, thereby reducing their intensity.

Creating space is an essential third step to emotional mindfulness. The reason emotions can often become so overwhelming is because they appear so close to us, leaving no space between us and the emotions. When we say we are angry or hurt, we imply that *we* are the emotion itself. It is akin to a hand covering our eyes, preventing us from seeing anything. In reality, emotions arise within us, and only when we practise being mindful of them, do we notice the difference. Observing our emotions suggests that our awareness of them is greater than the emotion itself. This shifts the perspective about the emotion being rigid and permanent, realising it is transient.

All these insights help reduce the intensity of strong emotions. As Victor E. Frankl noted, the space between stimulus and response grants us the power to choose our response. Practicing mindfulness and being aware of our emotions fosters the habit of creating this space. Neuropsychologist Donald O. Hebb coined the phrase 'Neurons that wire together fire together,' explaining how repeated actions become imprinted in our neural memory.

Tara Bennett-Goleman calls this space the 'magic quarter second'. While the situation may remain the same, labelling and observing it applies brakes to the emotional response.

The next step is to stay with the emotions. One cannot overstate the importance of simply staying with the emotions and feelings. We have an extremely low tolerance to awkward feelings and emotions, and we push it away at its first hint. The practice of mindfulness increases our ability to stay with our emotions and feelings.

Only by becoming adept at staying with our emotions do we gain the valuable insight that our emotions aren't as permanent and dense as we believe. They ebb and flow, coming and going, but only if we allow them to do so by developing the ability to stay with them. It's only when we're capable of staying with our discomfort and attending to it that we can move beyond it.

The final step is the anatomy of an emotion. Neuroscientist Jill Bolte Taylor's pioneering work has clearly demonstrated the nature of our emotions and their anatomy. She suggests that an emotion, left alone, lasts only 90 seconds. When triggered by a thought, the brain releases chemicals that surge through the body, creating a physiological response. Within 90 seconds, the chemical components of the emotion dissipate from the blood, and the chemical reaction ends. If the emotion persists beyond that, it's because we have allowed the circuit to run by replaying it with our thoughts and memories.

This insight offers us a means to free ourselves from the tyranny of strong emotions. As Pema Chödrön explains, if we mindfully become receptive to the sensation or emotion without dwelling on the story or thoughts behind it, we can flush it out of the system. The steps include acknowledging the feeling, being completely present and open to it, feeling it completely, but discarding the storylines and thoughts about it.

While it may not completely pass within the magic 90-second span, it will soon dissolve. Start with milder sensations like irritation or uneasiness, gradually moving on to more powerful emotions. When you experience a negative or uncomfortable emotion, explore it instead of pushing it away or distracting yourself. Sit with it mindfully, without judgement and be fully present with it.

Rosenberg Reset

This revolutionary comprehension of the 90-second rule has been eloquently outlined by psychologist Joan Rosenberg in her book, *90 Seconds to a Life You Love: How to Master Your Difficult Feelings to Cultivate Lasting Confidence, Resilience, and Authenticity*. Here, she proposes a three-step process called the 'Rosenberg Reset'.

1. Make the choice to be present, to be aware of, and in touch with your moment-to-moment experience as far as possible.

2. Acknowledge your willingness to deal with or tolerate these eight unpleasant feelings: Sadness, shame, helplessness, anger, embarrassment, disappointment, frustration, and vulnerability.

3. Move through these eight unpleasant feelings by riding one or more 90-second waves of bodily sensations. The physical sensations, such as warm cheeks, pounding

heart, or a pit in the stomach, serve as the body's way of communicating our emotions. Riding out both the physical sensations and the associated emotions is an essential part of the Rosenberg Reset. It's also essential to understand that we often blame ourselves for our emotions and feelings. When sadness arises, we immediately chastise ourselves, thinking, 'Maybe I'm doing something wrong and that's why I am feeling this' or 'If only I did everything right, I would not be having these feelings.' Such self-criticism only exacerbates the emotions. We must first understand that there is nothing wrong with experiencing uncomfortable emotions. Emotions, feelings, and thoughts come and go, and all we need to do is to accept them with compassion and care. Resistance to our feelings, thoughts, and emotions is the primary source of suffering. The formula to keep in mind is:

Suffering = pain (emotion, thought, feeling) x resistance.

If an emotion or thought feels uncomfortable, we resist it. Before we know it, a simple feeling amplifies into suffering. Acceptance of feelings and emotions enables them to remain a temporary source of discomfort.

Felt Sense of Emotion

Working mindfully with our emotions helps to have a felt sense of them. Emotions almost always generate physical sensations. These can be quite intense, which is why most people avoid experiencing them. Unless we tend to them and feel them, the exploration is incomplete. The axiom, 'feel it to heal it' perfectly summarises this concept.

David I. Rome, the author of *Your Body Knows the Answer* and creator of Mindful Focusing, describes felt senses as paradoxical. They are always present tend to go unnoticed unless they become intense. Developing the ability to feel our emotions may require some practice. As we gradually bring our awareness towards our bodies, we may learn to recognise these felt senses. They often have a location, shape, texture, or other tangible qualities, such as tightness in the neck or shoulders, a fluttering sensation in the chest, a racing the heart, or a rumbling belly.

Another important aspect is learning to suspend the narrative thought patterns to access the non-conceptual realm of direct experience. Our storylines are an interpretation of our experiences but not the experiences themselves. The finger pointing to the moon should not be confused with the moon itself.

To make direct contact with our felt experience, we must release the storyline delve beneath it to precisely discern how the body is experiencing the emotion. The felt sense lies beneath the emotional surface. We take gentle steps to first locate the feeling within the body, whether in the chest or belly, and then proceed to wholly engage with the feeling without the accompanying thoughts and narratives.

To get started, we can ask ourselves a few questions. Tara Brach often recommends asking, 'What am I unwilling to feel?' We then pause, take a step back, locate the feeling in our body, fully immerse ourselves in it. Since these feelings can be uncomfortable, we often resist engaging with them, making this question a valuable tool for leaning into the emotions.

David Rome suggests asking, 'What demands my attention right now?' Sometimes, when we stay with these feelings, insights may emerge as to why certain emotions have persisted for years. Our inability to stay with these emotions for an extended period is often the reasons they linger.

It's crucial to realise that at their core, emotions are energy and hold no inherent positivity nor negativity. It's our thoughts about them that construct the stories in our minds. Stripped of all thoughts and mental narratives, emotions are mere raw sensations, akin to a headache or toothache. It's the thoughts and stories that fan these sensations, transforming a small flame into an inferno. The lesson is to simply stay with the experience without generating a narrative, being present and receptive to the emotional itself.

Transmutation of Emotions

Joan Rosenberg also discusses a crucial but less-understood aspect of emotions—the transmutation of feelings. She explains that we often take the most challenging emotion for us to bear and express it as another feeling. Men frequently grapple with softer emotions like sadness, disappointment, or vulnerability and instead express them as anger, frustration, stress, irritability, or rage. Women may struggle with harder emotions, such as anger or frustration, and express them as hurt, disappointment, sadness, or tearfulness.

She also points out that some individuals may have a default mode for expressing emotions, consistently responding with the same emotion, regardless of the actual feeling. For instance, someone may experience sadness even when the underlying emotion is resentment or fear. For others, it may be perpetual anger or irritation. Such individuals often struggle with managing difficult emotions. Many people use anxiety to mask other uncomfortable feelings. Anxiety can seem more socially acceptable than the messier and more uncomfortable emotions. The key is to be mindful and aware of our true feelings, refraining from using emotional substitutes like irritation, anger, or anxiety as a cover-up.

In her book *The Greatest Secret*, Rhonda Byrne posits that any negative emotion or feeling, such as anger, fear, disappointment, or irritation, arises because these feelings have been unconsciously buried or suppressed for years. They now seek an outlet for release by exploiting external events as triggers. While we may believe that the trigger is the cause of our fear or anger, the actual source of the emotion is internal. Therefore, the readiness to react with fear hinges on the extent of pre-existing fear within us, ready to be triggered by a stimulus. This theory underscores how awareness of our emotions and feelings and a willingness to let them flow can facilitate healing.

Practising RAIN

The 'RAIN' practice is highly effective for managing strong emotions. This acronym was originally coined by Michele Macdonald and is often used by Tara Brach in her mindfulness sessions. Comprising of four steps, it can initially be done separately but must eventually be combined once mastered.

Recognise: The 'R' signifies recognizing the emergence of an emotion. Simply acknowledge its presence, which helps reduce its intensity.

Acceptance: The 'A' stands for acceptance. Permit the emotion to exist without attempting to push it away or suppress it. Resistance to the emotion is often the primary issue. Ask yourself, 'Can I allow the emotion to be there without trying to change it?' Acknowledge that there may be times when acceptance is challenging.

Investigate: The 'I' involves investigating the feeling as discussed earlier. Examine how the emotion manifests in the body. Identify its location, such as clenching, tightness, or heaviness in the chest or belly. Then, be present with it, mindfully observing the sensations without engaging in thoughts or commentary.

Nurture or Non-Identification: 'N' encourages allowing the emotion space while detaching from it in a non-judgmental manner. Non-identification means not taking emotions personally, creating separation between the emotion and oneself.

Emotional Alchemy

When we completely surrender to our suffering and emotions, we transform these intense feelings. Eckhart Tolle emphasises that any deep suffering or calamity is an opportunity for transformation. In *The Power of Now*, he advises, 'Become an alchemist. Transmute base metal into gold, suffering into consciousness, disaster into enlightenment.'

In my journey with emotions like despair, heartbreak, and loss, I experienced this alchemical transformation. Starting with profound suffering and concluding with an inexplicable sense of peace ignited my passion to understand the process deeply and assist others. This book is, in many ways, a product of that exploration.

Educationist and psychotherapist Tara Bennet-Goleman beautifully explains this process in her book *The Alchemy of Emotions*. She suggests that while the historical alchemists were believed to transmute lead into gold though a magical philosopher's stone, the lead and gold were, in many ways, metaphors for our internal transformation through presence and awareness. She likens our typical state of mind to coal and clear awareness, stillness, and presence to a diamond. Mindfulness, like alchemy, involves accepting emotional states as they are without attempting to modify or reject them. Emotional alchemy allows the potential for turmoil to blossom into peace and clarity, the undesirable into the desirable.

Psychotherapist and author Miriam Greenspan deals with emotional alchemy brilliantly in her soulful book *Healing of the Dark Emotions*. Having faced intense grief after the loss of her child, she shares her journey of pain, healing, and recovery. She describes emotional alchemy as the conscious flow of emotional information and energy. Emotional flow is about tolerating the energy of grief, fear, and despair in the body and allowing the wisdom of these emotions to unfold. Miriam outlines the three basic skills needed to deal with and transform the dark energies to gratitude, faith and joy. These are: Attending, befriending, and surrendering.

a. Attending is to sense the emotions with focussed awareness and name them. When we can focus our awareness on emotional energy in this manner, it offers us an opportunity to turn adversity into learning.

b. Befriending emotional energy is an extension of attending to it. In befriending the dark emotions, we let them be, not trying to suppress, dispel, deny, or analyse them.

c. Surrendering is about allowing the emotional energy to flow to its end point. It's being fully present to emotional energy and letting it pass through the body. A basic axiom of surrender is 'to let it go, you have to let it flow.' You can't fully let go of a dark emotion until you've experienced its truth. You surrender not by moving away from what hurts but by moving into it with awareness as protection. Mindful awareness and acceptance are the balms to heal pain, thereby turning poison into medicine.

Emotional alchemy is not merely a theoretical concept; it's a practical approach. Life often provides us with challenging and painful situations. A close friend of mine found himself in a perilous situation involving a clandestine affair and potential divorce to surrender to his emotions completely. He was deeply remorseful and longed for his wife to forgive him. I asked him to surrender to the situation as only in a state of complete acceptance can transmutation of emotions and alchemy can take place. Acknowledging and accepting his feelings without conditions and with humility allowed for the transformation of emotions. His scepticism transformed into hope as he followed this path.

A few weeks later he informed me that he could feel a shift within and surrendering to his emotions was cathartic. The situation outside was not improving much, but within himself he could experience a stillness that he had never envisaged under the circumstances. His wife was still deeply hurt, but he was hopeful that with perseverance and patience the situation could still be salvaged. He had surrendered to the outcome and was willing to accept whatever his wife decided with humility.

Inner Alchemists

We all possess the potential to be inner alchemists, capable of turning moments of confusion into insightful clarity through the right awareness tools. By practising mindfulness of emotions, we stop seeing feelings like irritation, resentment, or frustration as obstacles; rather, we embrace all aspects of this experience as the path itself. As Pema Chödron suggests, 'Feelings like disappointment, anger, and jealousy are messengers that show us with terrifying clarity exactly where we are stuck.'

We can slowly build our mindfulness muscles by pausing and asking ourselves, time to time, what we are feeling in the moment. Just like we log in and check our Instagram notifications from time to time, it is essential to check in on our feeling notifications, too. Learning to feel our body from within is something we are not used to doing, but it can be a transformative tool. It can help us open up and say 'yes' to all our feelings, however disturbing they may be, in a non-judgemental, compassionate manner without trying to modify or get rid of them.

In conclusion, Amoda Maa's words resonate: 'The darkness arises from your depth, and when you are ready, it will inform you of a much vaster you. A you that has the capacity to embrace and feel and allow the movement of all energies. And if you don't identify with these energies, but simply allow their movement, you will see that who you are is aliveness itself. . . . My friend, open your heart and let the light shine through the cracks. It is the light of being. And you are that.'

Practices

- Allow a feeling or emotion to be there as it is without trying to alter it. Try to see if you can have a felt sense of any feeling. What does anger or frustration feel like in your body?

- Practise staying with some strong emotion for half a minute or so. Can you stay with the raw discomfort of sadness, or loneliness for a few seconds without trying to suppress them?

- Ask yourself the question from time to time: 'What am I unwilling to feel?' Check in within yourself in between and ask: 'What am I feeling now?' or 'What is going on inside me now?'

- The 90-second rule. Whenever you experience an emotion of moderate intensity, say anger, or disappointment can you simply stay with the felt feeling and see how long it may last if you don't create any mental stories around it?

- Use the RAIN method with any kind of discomfort: Recognise the emotion in your body. Accept the emotion. Investigate it by trying to locate it in any part of the body and be present with it. Non-identification—letting there be space for the emotion to be and go away.

- Observe when you are resisting a feeling or emotion by not wanting it to be there or trying to push it away. How does it feel when you are resisting? How does it feel when you let it be?

- See if you can welcome feelings or emotions even if they are uncomfortable. Can you let there be room for all emotions and feelings?

- Notice if there are feelings that you commonly transmute. Maybe you feel anxious or irritated a lot, and actually it may be a cover for some other emotion like sadness or disappointment. Be curious about your common feelings.

- See if you can practice the alchemy of emotions using the steps. This way a strong emotion can be transformed by attending, befriending, and surrendering. But if the emotion is too strong or painful, you may need to sit with a therapist rather than practice it alone.

- Ask yourself what wants your attention right now? Which part of your body needs attention?

- Try staying with feelings of boredom or restlessness even for a few seconds. Then gradually you may increase it. You may notice how these feelings change over time, varying in intensity and even fading away if left alone.

- Practise being with an emotion without labelling it sadness, despondency, or frustration. Simply notice and be with it without labelling it as negative or unpleasant or judging it for being there.

6

EXPLORING 'WHO AM I?'

*'The place you are looking for is the place from which
you are looking.'*
—**Mooji**

It was the culmination of a grand ceremony. The graduation night had finally arrived, and we were awaiting our turn to be given the graduation degree with mounting excitement. For most of the 60 of us who were graduating that night, it was a dream come true. A dream that began many years ago when we aspired to become doctors, following two years of rigorous preparation for the entrance exams. The euphoria of getting into our dream college was soon replaced by the nervousness and elation of a new environment, the fear and excitement of ragging, and the bewildering introduction to anatomy classes.

The next four-and-a-half years went by in a haze, and eventually, all we could remember was cramming desperately for our final exams, hoping against hope that we would pass. Finally, the day had arrived when were to formally receive the medical degree. 'Doctor Saroj Dubey', a new chapter had begun for me, and a new identity that would follow me like a faithful shadow for the rest of my life. Whenever anyone introduced me, it was as a doctor, and when I wrote my name, there was often a trace of pride in the prefix, reminding me of all that I had achieved and who I was.

Never in my wildest dreams did I ever think that one day I would be grappling with this very question of my identity, and it would become almost an obsession for me to find the answer to the ancient question: 'Who am I?'

I cannot be sure when I first heard the word meditation and got interested in it. Probably in 2005 when we were undergoing rigorous training in gastroenterology, and I had to oscillate between taking care of the family and managing residential duties. Meditation seemed a promising tool to relieve me of the stress I was undergoing. However, the biggest obstacle was how to squeeze in time for it.

It was at this juncture that I chanced to read *The Monk Who Sold his Ferrari* by Robin Sharma. It was a fascinating book, and the one line that really caught my attention was his description of a man driving through a highway in a hurry to reach somewhere, his petrol tank hovering around the empty mark. However, he refused to stop to fill his tank because he felt he had no time to lose. This really set me thinking.

We have to take out the time to fill our tank first and replenish ourselves; otherwise, everything is in vain. From that day, whenever I thought that I had no time for myself, be it for meditation, self-nourishment, self-improvement, or exercise, I would remember these words and invariably find the time.

I felt a sense of ease, calm, and relaxation when I started meditating. I experimented with various methods, including concentration, Transcendental Meditation, and calm abiding, looking for the method that suited me best. My purpose at that time was quite clear; it was mainly a stressbuster and relaxation without the real desire for diving in deep. However, I also noticed that the effects would wear off slowly as I got off from the cushion. My next breakthrough came when I chanced upon Eckhart Tolle's *The Power of Now*, and it was a revelation that not being present was taken to be a totally normal state of being in our hectic lives.

It was then that I started mindfulness meditation and found it very satisfying. Although fascinated by Eckhart's teachings and my meditation practices and wanting to dive deeper, I was still caught up with my role of establishing myself as a consultant and getting some family time. Books and spirituality were still a luxury, which I relegated for retirement or some other distant future. There was no time for serious spirituality right now; there was much more important and practical work to be done. But life has many surprises in store for us, and Rashmi's incident came like a thunderstorm that threatened to pull my life apart.

The question uppermost in my mind was whether life was just about our luck and fortune, a mere matter of chance? I had to know the truth.

This quest made me wander from gurus to books and to seek the counsel of teachers who had apparently seen the truth. I had read about enlightened beings, and it seemed to me that being enlightened meant an end to all seeking. So, I was desperately in search of an enlightened master to guide me properly. After much soul-searching and exploration, I found that the non-duality teachings based on the Advaita Vedanta tradition seemed to most resonate with me.

The central premise of this philosophy is that there is nothing other than consciousness. Or in other terms, all is consciousness. All creation is fused into the warp and weft of the Creator. The 5000-year-old Upanishads, ecstatic declarations of Oneness by realised sages, are synonymous with Advaita. The great sage, Adi Shankaracharya, who lived in 800 AD, is one of its chief proponents.

Of modern sages, none is more respected than Ramana Maharshi who, in the middle of the 20th century, emerged with his method of self-enquiry about our true nature. It seemed apparent to me that if one had to find out the cause of his or her suffering, it was imperative to know the reality of who was it that was suffering? So, the all-important questions were:

- Who am I really? What is my true nature? Is there more to me than what I think, see, feel in my day-to-day life?
- Is there a person or doer behind all the actions that we undertake?

It made sense to me that if I were to find out the answers to these questions, a lot of my doubts could be clarified. Many of you may find them to be rather obvious superficial questions. In fact, I remember when I was asked this for the first time by a teacher, I thought to myself, 'Oh, please, come on, I am this person Saroj, a doctor, the one standing before you, what else is there to think about?'

But when one starts the process of inquiry, then the layers begin to unpeel. The wisdom and teachings of enlightened masters like Mooji, a spiritual teacher based in Portugal; Rupert Spira, an English spiritual teacher and author of the Direct Path based in Oxford; Adyashanti, an American spiritual teacher and author from the San Francisco Bay Area; Eckhart Tolle, and Anantaji (Ananta Garg, also lovingly called 'Father'), a disciple of Sri Mooji, guided me on this journey that is continuing. I devoured books with an intensity I had last shown during my medical entrance exams, and attended meetings and retreats wherever possible.

I remember going to meet Anantaji in Bangalore and telling him about the entire Rashmi incident, my guilt, my torment, and my desperation to seek answers, and he asked me gently, 'First find out who is this person "I" that you keep referring to all the time? Who is this person who seems to be in so much suffering and is so desperate for answers? Let's try to find out his nature first.'

When we start the process of self-enquiry, we begin with the belief that we are this complex interplay of body–mind called Saroj, in my case, or it may be Ramesh, or Gayatri. We feel that behind this body-mind is a miniature me (a sort of small Saroj) who is the main controller and decision-maker of the actions that we undertake. 'Look and see whether it is true,' exhorts Mooji. Thus, we look for this person with an aim to negate that which is not true and discover that which is unchanging and ever present.

I cannot be that which I observe because if I am able to observe something, then obviously it is at a distance from me and hence it cannot be me. A weighing machine can weigh everything except itself. Since I can observe my body, my head, face, and arms, I am not the body.

We have this strong conditioning and belief since early childhood that we are this body, but we realise on searching that the body is a vehicle for us to experience this world. It is not what we are at the core.

The mind is more complex, but there is no separate entity called the mind; it is made of all thoughts, emotions, and sensations. But when we sit down and really observe, we discover that we can observe our thoughts and emotions, too. All that is passing through our mind is observable, and so I am not my thoughts, emotions, or mind either. The voice in our head sounds like us and seems to be like us, but it is not what we are. It also is our mind, issuing a background commentary about every action we take: 'I am too slow; I am not smart enough; I am not good enough; I am the best; I have to keep up with the others; I can't do it; I don't deserve to be happy.' These are all thoughts, beliefs, and the commentary given by the mind, but thoughts arise and disappear. These thoughts have a strong 'I' belief, and so with every thought, there is an 'I' attached, giving rise to the belief in our separate self. The question to ask, therefore, is: 'What is it that stays behind, that is aware of all the thoughts and feelings?'

So, who is this person behind every action and movement of mine? When I look with awareness, I cannot find any person or entity called Saroj. Throughout our life, we believe in this separate self, ego, or psychological self, which is a description of this mind-body complex that we take to be the real 'I'. And when we inquire deeply, we find that it is not real. There is simply awareness of the body, thoughts, emotions, and sensations. Simply awareness, no person, no entity, no miniature me, but everything is floating in awareness. As Mooji suggests, 'A person is what you experience; it is not what you are.' All these clusters of beliefs and thoughts, memories, and feelings form the illusion of a separate self or entity. Our thoughts and beliefs that we are a separate person are what create all our suffering, explains Rupert Spira.

Unveiling Our True Self

What is the mystery of our true nature? We are not our body but that which is aware of our body. We are not our thoughts or emotions but the one aware of them. So, who is the real 'I' that is unchanging, aware, and omnipresent?

'You are awareness itself,' reveals Rhonda Byrne in *The Greatest Secret*. Only the presence of awareness is real and unchanging. Awareness is what we really are, our true identity, the missing link. It is so close to us that we have missed it throughout our lives. In his book *Shift into Freedom*, Loch Kelly suggests we don't recognise awake awareness because it is:

> So close you can't see it,
> So subtle your mind can't understand it,
> So simple you can't believe it,
> So good you can't accept it.

Awareness is conscious of every single life experience we have. Our mind, thoughts, and body are not aware of our life, but rather it is awareness that is conscious of our mind, body, and thoughts.

The answer to 'who am I?' does not always strike us out of the blue, though it may be a sudden recognition for many by an act of grace. For many others like me, it is a gradual unfolding of layers. However and whenever it arrives, it will undoubtedly change our perception towards life. Sri Ramana Maharshi puts it eloquently: 'The question "Who am I?" is not really meant to get an answer, it is meant to dissolve the questioner.'

Awareness is like the vast ocean, boundless and expansive. It is akin to the space in the room that never voices its preference for specific objects or people. Our true nature is like this boundless ocean, able to welcome all that it touches, unpleasant thoughts, disturbing emotions, or painful sensations. There is space for all.

Presence

Eckhart Tolle prefers to use the word 'presence', which is almost the same as awareness. He warns readers that presence is not what you think it is: You can't think about it and the mind can't understand it, so don't objectify it. Presence is manifested when the mind is still, and it is presence itself that is aware of and appreciates beauty, majesty, and the sacredness of nature. Eckhart explains that when you become conscious of being, being or awareness becomes conscious of itself. When being becomes conscious of itself, that's presence. It is liberating to gain access to this formless realm of ourselves. We can call it the unmanifested, being, awareness, the source, or I am. It is the realm of deep stillness and peace as also of joy and intense aliveness.

Tolle describes the various portals into the unmanifested. Deep, dreamless sleep is a portal, but to truly understand it we need to enter it consciously. The main portals that he talks about are:

a. The Inner Body: We can use our inner body as a portal to access the unmanifested.

b. The Now: When we are intensely present, there is dissolving of psychological time and we are connected to the unmanifested, the source.

c. Cessation of Thinking: A gap in continuous thinking opens a portal to presence, which can occur during meditation or when mental commentary ceases, such as when observing nature, beauty, or hearing a joke. Nature and beauty often serve as doorways to Beingness.

d. Surrender: Releasing mental-emotional resistance to the present moment is another gateway to the unmanifested.

e. Silence: Eckhart advises seeking the silence from which sounds originate and return to. Prioritise inner silence over external noise, as it leads to stillness of the mind, opening a portal.

f. Space: Like silence, Eckhart strongly advocates one to be more aware of space than objects. All our attention is taken up by objects, but when we pay attention to space, a portal opens up inside us.

I Am

How do we normally introduce ourselves? 'Hi, I am Saroj, Niloufer, or Rajiv. I am a doctor, lawyer, engineer.' Or we identify our emotional states as: 'I am happy, sad, or irritated.' So, there is always something attached to 'I am'. This becomes our identity—I am a husband, a father, an Indian.

But what is that which comes before all this? Who or what is it that knows that I am a doctor, husband, father, or Indian? What is this first sense of knowing when we enter the body? It is the I am, pure presence or Beingness, our true identity. How do we know that we exist? If, due to some neurological illness, our entire memory and identity were lost (which is medically possible), then what is it that remains of us? We do not cease to exist, do we? We exist, we are, we are present as the I am.

So, when we begin searching for our true nature by going backward, this 'I am' is our beacon guide to our true identity. In Zen circles, there is a koan that asks, 'What is your face like before you were born?'

Mooji guides us to explore our true identity . . . this sense of I am. He asks us to go to that feeling or sense that is beyond any thought, label, or identity. Before we know anything, we know that we exist—I am. This is our first knowing, consciousness announcing itself. He guides us to sit with this felt sense or intuition of I am. Simply put, place your attention on this I am sense without attaching any stories or identity.

Mooji suggests that the more we linger with the sense of 'I am', the greater our sense of openness and peace becomes. He recommends abiding in it and cautions that thoughts will inevitably arise, and the mind may attempt to hinder our progress, questioning the purpose of these efforts. 'Don't engage with the mind,' he advises. 'Simply abide and remain with the "I am" feeling".

Analysing the Structure of Objects

During these enquiries, I was more drawn to the 'direct path' as opposed to the 'progressive path'. The promise of being able to have a glimpse of our true nature directly, without having to go through a lifetime of meditation and progressive purification, was quite irresistible, which is the hallmark of the direct path.

Most of us have been brought up with the concept that there is a subject 'I' who observes an object, which can be something we see, hear, or think. We shall investigate whether this model is true. Sit comfortably and be aware of any sounds in your vicinity, perhaps the sound of a bell. Simply be aware of the bell's sound arising and fading. Then ask yourself: 'Is there a bell separate from the sound? Is there a separate entity called a bell waiting to be heard or in your direct experience can you just hear the bell?'

If we are honest and open about it, we may realise that all we can experience of the bell is hearing, it is only when we refer to our thoughts or memory can we label the sound a bell. There doesn't appear to be a stand-alone object called the bell.

a. *Is the hearing outside or inside of us or at any distance from us?*

Our thoughts might suggest the presence of a distant sound, but in our immediate perception, we only encounter the act of hearing the sound right here, with no spatial separation from our current location.

b. *Is there a separate hearing apart from the awareness of it?*

Having conformed that our entire sensory experience pertains solely to what we hear, we realise that the essence of hearing boils down to the awareness of it.

Rupert Spira illustrates this beautifully with the example of the movie screen and the variety of images and activities going on in the form of a movie. The screen may be hidden from view but pervades the entire movie and images. In fact, it may be appropriate to say that there is nothing else to the movie than the screen that contains it. There is no separate movie other than the screen, the movie cannot be separated from the screen.

Similarly, our real nature as awareness pervades all our experiences of seeing, hearing, tasting, or smelling, but we often overlook this obvious fact. In fact, one can say that all there is to the experience of seeing, hearing, tasting, or smelling is the awareness of it.

William Blake was probably implying this when he said: 'If the doors of perception were cleansed every thing would appear to man as it is, Infinite.'

The Headless Way

The nature of our reality is also demonstrated beautifully in a series of experiments by Douglas Harding, author of *The Headless Way*. He describes the method to be a turning of our attention through an angle of 180 degrees. Our attention is normally directed outwards, at an object. If I am looking at you, what happens if I turn my attention to where I am looking from? Where is the bow from which this arrow of attention is being shot from?

What we find when we direct our attention 180 degrees is a fantastic revelation. I cannot see anything, here there is no face, no head, but an empty space. For instance, I am pointing my finger at various objects—a chair, a person, a table, and then I point my finger to where I imagine my face is. We will find that there is no object there in reality; in fact, our thoughts and minds project a head at that place.

We have been conditioned to believe that we are a 'boy' or 'girl' with a face, and we believe that since our sensory organs of seeing and hearing are located in the head, our head is the source of who or what we are. A baby has no realisation of its body parts; it is pure awareness. This is our true nature, but we gradually outgrow it and believe ourselves to be that person we see in the mirror.

However, as we come closer and closer to ourselves, we can't find any of these features that we have always believed ourselves to be. We are simply a pure space of awareness.

These techniques can be performed and verified by anyone regardless of meditation training or spiritual belief. It is simply an open and new way of seeing things. Once it's noticed, it can change the way we look at things. We believe that we are looking with our two eyes, and that is what we see in another person. But from that space from where I am looking, which is above my neck, there is just one view, seeing from an open space. And if I am able to see that instead of my head is a large open space, then where is the distinction between me and the other person?

Similarly, if we switch to hearing, then we realise there is a vast empty space of awareness, and sounds are passing through this space. All kinds of sensations are being experienced through this aware space. This is what all the spiritual masters teach us: We are all interconnected and our nature is pure awareness.

Thus, instead of simply taking it at face value, we can test it for ourselves and see what we find. At the very least, this realisation will prompt us to consider the possibility that our perceptions and self-conceptions may not be as accurate as we've assumed. We are not merely confined to the rigid, corporeal identity we've held, but instead, there exists a profound expansiveness within us that merits thorough examination and exploration.

Resting as Awareness

I distinctly remember a hot, bright sunny day in January in Goa when, after a few rounds of dipping in the ocean, I simply laid down on my back on the hot sand, looking up at the vast expanse of the clear blue sky, hearing the sounds of the waves and raising my head to look at the never-ending, vast magnificent blue sea. I don't know how long I lay there on the sand, but the feeling was glorious and delicious, and I had no words to describe it.

The feeling was of a deep stillness, peace, happiness, joy, aliveness, spaciousness, and a distinct feeling of extreme well-being. A few months later, I remember reading an excerpt in a book that described our true nature, and it was the same— spacious, alive, sense of well-being, joyful, and I realised that on that sunny day in Goa I had accidentally stumbled upon this glimpse of pure awareness. Visiting Goa during the winters has now become an annual affair.

In a talk between spiritual teacher David Bingham and Hale Dwoskin, founder of the Sedona method, they called this state as pure awareness. We can experience glimpses of it in our daily lives.

I often stop the car, especially when the sun is bright, and sit still for some time. Or when I meditate, I simply sit, allowing all sounds, sensations, and feelings to come and go. Consider taking a nature walk, being amidst lush greenery, or the vast sky or near water bodies. We can do this as a practice from time to time to develop a taste of our true nature of pure, effortless awareness.

Enlightenment as Goal

During my journey as a seeker, I attended numerous retreats, and meetings, where I mixed with fellow seekers who were all trying to find their true nature and ways to end suffering. It amazed me to see that there were so many from across the world who were eager for answers. Among my colleagues, friends, and relatives in India, whenever I brought up the subject of spirituality or awakening, the topic was either made light of or brushed aside. I may be wrong in my conclusion, but I feel that foreigners are thirstier for truth, and often find their answers in India.

I also observed that for many spiritual aspirants, enlightenment or awakening becomes a goal. The energy and attention that was earlier expended on gaining material goals had now been transferred to a spiritual goal. It often becomes a destination to reach at some distant future. For some, it must be reached at all costs in order to feel happy and fulfilled. I, too, had booked a seat on this spiritual bus and was travelling with zeal and passion, till the realisation came that there was nowhere to go but here.

Anthony de Mello illustrates: 'The spiritual quest is a journey without distance. You travel from where you are right now to where you have always been.' Hence, each moment is cherished, and the aim is to say 'yes' to whatever arrives in the moment. I love teaching mindfulness reading about people who have achieved enlightenment and have an awakening experience. It has become a habit to read a few pages each day and watch a couple of videos about our true nature, creativity, joy happiness, and inner growth. I believe that life is our best guru, and it will always provide us with opportunities to learn, grow, and expand. All we need is to be open to life at each moment.

There is no demarcation between a spiritual and material life, and we don't need to sacrifice anything other than that which doesn't resonate with us. When we get a taste of our real nature there is a lightness and expansiveness in our daily living. We don't need to exclude anything at all. In fact, our involvement in life becomes even more intimate because we see how we are all interconnected, so there is no feeling of 'us vs them' anymore.

Practices

- Are you aware? Pose this question to yourself and observe what unfolds. Where do you turn to seek the answer? Take note of your responses. What surfaces when you inquire, 'Who am I?' Is it your body or your mind? Who are you without any belief, label, or thought? If you were to lose all your memories, who would remain? What forms your identity?

- Immerse yourself in the experience and intuition of 'I am'. Simply abide in the sensation of 'I am' without appending anything further.

- Practise listening to sound, pure listening.

- Picture yourself as a newborn, gazing at an object for the very first time. What do you perceive when you look at an apple? Is it not merely colours and the act of seeing it? See through the unconditioned eyes of an infant.

- Practise recognising awareness, unadulterated awareness devoid of thoughts. Sustain the state of open awareness.

- Practise simply being, with no agenda, just exist. Sit and allow whatever unfolds to occur. Practise for 3–5 minutes and remain attentive to any restlessness or agitation.

- Attempt to be non-aware. Is it feasible not to be aware? Can you become unaware? Even when you deactivate all sensations, what is cognisant of that?

- Can you cultivate the practice of embracing everything within your experience? Any thought, any emotion, any sensation. Is it viable to wholeheartedly accept and permit it all?

- Create a list of activities that invigorate you— dance, music, or sports. These serve as gateways to your essence. Engage in these activities more and allow whatever emerges to surface. Consider if joy doesn't solely reside in the activity but in your mind growing tranquil, permitting your awareness to savour itself.

- Examine your hand and start swaying it in all directions. Your eyes may shift around as your hand moves. Is your awareness swaying too, or does it remain still?

- Point your finger in the direction of your head. What do you discern? Is it not sheer emptiness?

7

THOUGHTS: REAL BUT ILLUSORY

'Thoughts are like taxis. You get in, they take you for a ride,
and you are left with a bill to pay. Instead why not let
them drive by?'

—Gelong Thubten

I looked up at the distinguished gentleman who, along with his wife, anxiously awaited while I thoroughly reviewed all his reports—the ultrasound, endoscopy, CT scan, and blood reports. 'Mr Yashpal, there's no need to worry. All your reports are perfectly normal.' However, rather than feeling reassured, Mr Yashpal, a former professor at the Indian Institute of Technology (IIT), appeared unconvinced and disappointed, seeking an explanation for his persistent abdominal pain over the past eight months.

I gently suggested that he might be experiencing some anxiety and stress. His wife interjected forcefully, 'But we have no stress at all. We are comfortably retired, and our children are well settled abroad. What possible anxiety or worry could we have?'

This time, Mr Yashpal seemed contemplative. After a brief pause, he looked at me and said, 'You know, doctor, you could be right. It's true that we have nothing to worry about. But I just can't seem to stop thinking. I can't stop imagining that I may have an incurable disease. I used to take pride in my mind and my thinking abilities, but now it seems to be the source of my lack of peace.'

Identified With Thoughts

What Mr Yashpal shared is not uncommon. We are often so deeply identified with our thoughts that we find ourselves at their mercy. What is it about thoughts that entangle and overwhelm us?

Roughly speaking, we all have about 75,000 thoughts in our minds each day, with the majority being repetitive and recycled. For a significant part of my life, I was identified with my thoughts, and I couldn't conceive of any separation between me and my thoughts. They always seemed inseparable. Didn't René Descartes famously declare, 'I think therefore I am'?

As a diligent student, employing my mind for thinking and analysis was my most important tool, and questioning it appeared sacrilegious. It was only when I encountered the phrase 'You are not your thoughts' in *The Power of Now* that I was taken aback.

'Not my thoughts, but how can that be possible? It's preposterous,' I told myself. Everything I believe in, identify with, and my actions are based on my ability to think. And here was Eckhart, trying to convince me that I was not my thoughts.

He proceeded to discuss the voice in the head, running a constant commentary in the background: 'I am not good enough', 'what will people think of me?', 'how can he say that to me?', and so on. This voice has an opinion on everything along with a habit of judging and commenting on whatever is going on. Only when we become present and mindful can we see that our incessant thoughts, in the form of this voice in the head, do not define our essential selves. Of course, our thoughts are real, not imaginary. The vital question is: Are they true? Eckhart's remarkable statement drove me to explore the nature of thoughts, their reality, solidity, permanence, or lack thereof. It was only when I delved into my mindfulness meditation practice that I caught a glimpse of their true nature.

Initially, thoughts seemed to inundate my mind, relentlessly colliding without any breaks or space. They tumbled one after the other, leaving no room for anything else. But once I introduced a moment of stillness and silence, I could discerns a small gap between the thoughts.

The first time I experienced this was when I found myself stuck in a dreadful traffic jam. My mind was on overdrive: 'Oh no, I'll be very late, and the patients will start complaining. The VIP waiting to meet me will create a fuss.' Suddenly, I let go, recognising that since this was beyond my control, there was no point in dwelling on it.

In that sudden release, there was a pause in the ceaseless noise in my head, and to my surprise, I could observe my thoughts. *So, if I was able to observe these thoughts, I obviously wasn't the same as my thoughts.* This was a small 'eureka' moment, and I realised that this was what Eckhart referred to as the voice in the head. With this understanding, there was a slight shift towards calmness and space, despite the external chaos.

As my mindfulness practice deepened, I made further progress. When you sit with mindfulness, thoughts emerge from all directions. We simply need to be aware of them. If you feel stressed and anxious, you might even label them as fearful or anxious thoughts. By simply labelling them, we create a small space between us and our thoughts. Once this space is created, we realise that we are separate from our thoughts. This awareness diminishes the grip and influence of thoughts over us.

Remember Victor Frankl's quote? 'Between stimulus and response there is a space and in that space is the power to choose our response.' It was an enlightening moment of insight when I realised that thinking was only an aspect of my awareness. *Awareness does not require thoughts, but thoughts cannot exist in the absence of awareness.*

Awareness of Thoughts

We often overlook that our mind and thoughts act as a filter for how we perceive the world around us. Consider taking a leisurely walk in the park and enjoying nature. It won't be long before your mind starts to intrude with thoughts such as, 'I wonder what this flower is called?' or 'this park should be better maintained,' or 'it's not as good as the other park.' The charm and beauty that was present just moments ago begin to fade.

Undoubtedly, thoughts have a valuable role to play in our lives, but the issue lies in how we become entangled in them. Instead of comparing, labelling, and judging, we can allow things to be the way they are and experience things directly, free from filter of our minds. It's important to have control over the mind's switch button. Rather than becoming victims and slaves to our thoughts, we can use thinking as a creative and potent tool. This occurs when we experience moments of thought-free awareness in our everyday lives.

The Law of Attraction

How does all this impact our daily lives? Is it merely an interesting concept, or can it make a difference?

Well, it can fundamentally change the way we lead our lives because most of the time, we find ourselves under the rule and sway of our thoughts. They appear to govern us, but once we realise that thoughts come and go within awareness, we no longer need to be imprisoned by them.

Our thoughts are based on our conditioning, which is a combination of all that we have been taught to believe since childhood, along with our life's experiences. However, they are not omniscient by any means. We can pick and choose thoughts that are beneficial for us, and discard those that seem to pull us down.

There is no doubt that thoughts are powerful. I was deeply fascinated by the power of thoughts since reading about the 'Law of Attraction' in Rhonda Byrne's bestseller, *The Secret*. It had an enormous impact on me, making me realise how I had subscribed to limiting thoughts and beliefs and changing them was a huge part of my journey.

'I'm not creative' or 'I'm not attractive enough' were recurrent thoughts. It made a substantial difference when I ceased to adhere to them and consciously decided to be mindful of the nature of my thoughts and beliefs. Being aware of my thoughts empowered me to transform them into more empowering versions.

However, once I started practising mindfulness and delved deeper into the nature of the mind, I came to realise that while thoughts essential, they were not the source of our happiness and peace. In fact, our job was to follow our thoughts to their ultimate source. This source is the very wellspring of our existence, pure awareness, which resides at the heart of all our experiences.

To my delight, I discovered that Rhonda Byrne's latest book, *The Greatest Secret*, explores this very concept. It represents an evolution in her quest to unearth the origin from which all thoughts and beliefs originate. She has found that thoughts arise in the backdrop of awareness. She states that whether our experience is joyous or melancholic, whether we are filled with uplifting or distressing thoughts; freedom lies in recognising that at the heart of all these experiences is the aware presence, our true nature.

Is it True?

A powerful and highly practical method for exploring the nature of our thoughts is to use the approach devised by Byron Katie. Byron is an American spiritual teacher and author who began teaching a method of self-inquiry known as 'The Work' after realising that the cause of most of our suffering are unquestioned stressful thoughts. Once we delve into the core of our thoughts and question them, we gain the ability to penetrate the layers of our thoughts and beliefs.

Byron Katie's method involves questioning our thoughts using four inquiries when we encounter troubling thoughts:

- Is it true?
- Can you be absolutely certain that it is true?
- How do you react when you believe that thought?
- Who would you be without the thought?

To truly benefit from this, we need to maintain stillness and silence, meditating deeply on these questions rather than just thinking about the answers from a mental perspective. The mind tends to engage in logical debates and analysis, which not provide any freedom or insight. Each time we question our thoughts, we release the strength of our beliefs developed during childhood. We realise that we have clung to these thoughts for a long time, and they are the source of our anguish. The fascinating aspect is0020that they seem real but are actually not true.

When we say that thoughts are real but not true—as phrased by the Tibetan teacher Tsoknyi Rinpoche—it means that any narrative we hold about ourselves differs from the unfolding reality of who we are. Nonetheless, our beliefs consistently filter and interpret reality, causing us to mistake the stories about ourselves and the world for reality itself. This error is akin to confusing the map for the territory itself.

Consider, for instance, a common thought that haunts us from time to time, especially when we compare ourselves to our friends or colleagues: 'I am not earning enough.' We can examine this closely using Byron's method. When we ask ourselves if it's true, our immediate response might be: 'Yes, it appears to be true.' However, by doing so, we open the door to the possibility that there might be more to it, creating some space for inquiry.

We question again if we can be absolutely certain about the truth of this statement. Upon reflection, we might find ourselves less certain. It is only when we compare ourselves to our peers that we fall short. On an absolute level, we might be comfortable with our earnings, as most of our needs are easily met, and we may even have some savings left. To make a true comparison, we should consider those who earn less than us, which makes it hard to be absolutely sure of the initial statement's accuracy.

Moving on to the third question: How do we feel when we believe this statement? We may feel miserable, unhappy, and unmotivated. Physical sensations, such as a tightness in the chest or stomach, may accompany these negative emotions. We begin to notice a subtle resistance towards our work, as we feel it doesn't provide us with adequate compensation.

As for the final question about how we would feel without these limiting thoughts, the answer is clear: we would be happier, more grateful, motivated, and lighter. This is how we normally function, operating from a mindset of comparison and relativity, which leads to a sense of insufficiency, causing us to overlook are true blessings.

After understanding this approach and questioning and releasing thoughts about various subjects, I discussed it with a close friend who was dealing with issues concerning his teenage son, Vikrant. He found the exercise extremely helpful and later shared his insights with me. He often harboured the recurring thought that his son was lazy and irresponsible, especially when he observed Vikrant sleeping in late.

He decided to delve into this thought: 'Is it true? Can I know for certain that Vikrant was irresponsible and lazy?' My friend meditated on this for quite some time and realised that most of his beliefs were based on his preconceived notions about how he wanted his son to be, influenced by his own youthful efficiency and industriousness.

My friend confessed that most of his thoughts were rooted in the fear that Vikrant's lack of effort in his studies would result in poor exam performance, which could lead to him being perceived as a bad parent. Mentally, he compared Vikrant's performance to the children of his colleagues, which fuelled envy and feelings of inadequacy. He even went as far as envisioning Vikrant becoming a liability due to his perceived inability to excel academically and secure a decent job.

Thus, he realised that his assessment of Vikrant's irresponsibility was based on his own fears and anxieties, as well as his tendency to compare with others. This shift in perception led him to acknowledge that his son had his unique qualities, which he would share with the world when the time was right. Regarding Vikrant's 'laziness' and lack of effort, my friend began considering the possibility that it was Vikrant's life purpose to learn important lessons about diligence and responsibility.

Post this, he turned to the third question on how he felt when he believed that Vikrant was irresponsible. He immediately tensed. Agitation and non-acceptance permeated his being.

When he addressed the fourth question about how he would feel if he were free of this thought, there was an immediate lightness and joy within him, as he was free to love Vikrant and accept him the way he was—unconditionally and completely.

To hear my friend's ability to deconstruct his thoughts and beliefs was liberating. It is common for us to judge everyone around us, make comparisons, draw our own conclusions, and get upset in the process. However, life becomes simpler when we accept others as they are and drop our rigid beliefs. As coach Bobbi Chegwyn brilliantly suggests, 'Your perception of me is a reflection of you; my reaction to you is an awareness of me.'

Addiction to Thinking

Our creative or innovative thoughts are not under dispute. Thoughts are wonderful, creative, and potent when used properly, but the majority of our thoughts are repetitive, habitual, recycled, and compulsive.

Compulsive thinking is one of the biggest maladies of our time. We are under pressure to continuously keep thinking and worrying. We fear our problems will get out of hand if we don't worry enough. Somehow, there's a strange notion that if we worry and think hard enough, it will partially alleviate the problem. But does this happen? In fact, our habitual thoughts and worries prevent us from living a more open and free life.

Like any other addiction, compulsive thinking, too, is an addiction and equally injurious. We have forgotten how to create a gap in our thinking, since it has become synonymous with our identity. There is a joke about a person riding a horse, furiously speeding away, and his friend shouting, 'Hey, where are you going in such a tearing hurry?' The rider looks back desperately and shouts back, 'I'm not too sure, better ask the horse.'

In some ways this has become the story with our thoughts, too. Thoughts have a charge and drag us with their momentum. However, we can choose to step away from compulsive thinking. Thoughts might keep coming, but we don't need to entertain them. As Zen master Shunryū Suzuki suggests, 'Leave your front door and back door open. Allow your thoughts to come and go. Just don't serve them tea.'

Eckhart Tolle also suggests that we can practise being conscious and aware without thinking. We don't need to always label and judge things. We may see a scenery or image and simply be aware of it. This helps to gradually create a gap between thoughts. The more we practise using our senses and be aware without thinking, the easier it becomes to create this gap.

Is There a Thinker?

Hale Dwoskin, founder of the Sedona Training Associates, asks: Is there a thinker behind our thoughts, or do thoughts arise naturally in awareness? This is the most crucial distinction to make, and it is a life-changing revelation to distinguish between the two.

Let us explore this. Pause for a moment, be still and look at something. It could be any object, a table or the phone you are holding. When you see something, do your eyes say, 'I am seeing'? Or is it that once you have seen it, there is a thought that comes later and comments, 'I am seeing the phone.' Pause for a moment and notice this. Read it again.

Now you can switch to your hearing. Allow yourself to hear the sound of a car, or the chirping of birds. Pause for a few seconds. Does your ear tell you, 'I am hearing the sound'? Or is it that after the hearing, the thought creeps in to announce, 'I heard the sound of a car.' Repeat these experiments from time to time, and you will come to an important breakthrough. Hearing, seeing, touching, all take place in the background of an aware presence.

The thought comes in after that and says, 'I heard,' 'I saw,' creating the illusion that there is a person behind the perception. And what about thoughts themselves? Do we ever think a thought? We seem to believe so, but once again we can explore and see. Let a thought cross your mind.

Can you observe it? Was there someone behind who was creating this thought? We already explored earlier on that there is no person, but simply aware presence. So, we realise that thoughts come and go in the background of this never-changing awareness. It is a subsequent thought that comes in afterwards, claiming credit for the thinking. For instance:

Thought no. 1: 'I wonder what to have for breakfast?'
Thought no. 2: 'I think I'll have toast with coffee.'

Here it gives the illusion that a thinker is initiating the first thought and the second thought corroborates it. However, the first thought arises out of the blue and the second thought (based on one's choices and beliefs) enters to give the appearance that there is a thinker and chooser.

Don't Believe Your Next Thought

Many wise teachers offer a profound mantra to solve this problem of compulsive thinking. Renowned non-duality teacher Anantaji suggests, 'Don't believe your next thought.' American spiritual teacher Adyashanti, too, often underlines that the path to real freedom is to stop believing your thoughts. But what exactly do they mean?

We must stop identifying with thoughts because they represent a fractured reality, not the whole picture. For example, a thought may arise: 'I am not worthy or loveable enough,' and we start believing in this story. Through our conditioning, childhood memories, and experiences, this thought gradually solidifies into a dense, unshaken belief as if it were the gospel truth. We need to stop believing these stories and extricate ourselves from the network of fixed beliefs and impressions.

Founder of Dharmata Foundation, Anam Thubten, says that our thoughts are always colouring and defining reality.

When we step away from identification with thoughts, we are able to see life more directly, rather than through the lens of our belief systems. We experience the reality of the moment as it is, and not through the filter of thoughts. Much of our suffering is because of unwelcome thoughts.

When we encounter a traffic congestion on our way to work, our mind comes up with an angry thought, 'Oh no, this is horrible, the traffic constable doesn't know how to operate. Everyone is so irresponsible.' Eventually, we reinforce our belief that no one is responsible and conclude that our day is doomed. Notice how it all started with a single thought, a thought resisting the moment as it is. When we resist what is happening, it sets the stage for suffering. The moment we say yes to what is, we cease identifying with the resisting thoughts. Then, with awareness, we see directly what is happening and take appropriate actions.

The Separate Self Is a Thought

When we delve deeper into the nature of our reality, we come to a profound insight. We realise that this ego-based identity, this personal sense of I and me, is also a thought. Our entire life has been spent in service to this egoic 'I', this 'I' who is happy, sad, needy, lacking, and unfulfilled. The voice in our head, as discussed earlier, creates this narrative of 'I' and 'mine' right from childhood.

It is only when we look beyond this voice in our heads and the associated thoughts and emotions that we take a glimpse into spaciousness. We slowly peel the layers and identify this 'I'. We look at what is deeper than our thoughts and begin to see the presence, which is massive. We begin to see that this concept of a separate person and identity of 'I' is also a thought. A thought we have identified with our memories, emotions, conditioning, and belief systems. We come to recognise our true nature as presence awareness, and this so-called I we have believed to be the separate self, the thinker, the doer, is also discovered to be a thought that we have believed in strongly.

This belief causes us to struggle instead of moving along effortlessly, because this 'I' believes it is a separate, contracted, and fearful self that needs to defend itself and prove that it is right. Therefore, knowing that this voice in the head and the associated thoughts are not what we truly are is tremendously liberating and sets the stage for expansiveness and joy to enter our lives as opposed to lack and grasping.

This chapter is an invitation to explore the nature of our thoughts and beliefs, to be open to the possibility that our thoughts are not as solid as we may believe them to be. Perhaps the concepts seem a bit strange, but right now we can become mindful and aware of the thoughts running through our minds. Can we be aware of our thoughts, and by doing so create a gap between them? This is the crucial first step.

Gradually, we stop identifying with and believing in every thought. With the light of presence and awareness, we begin to understand how most of our thoughts have been planted in us from childhood and have become our identity. We can now hold each thought to scrutiny and question whether they are really true. Is it reality or merely a representation of reality?

When we are willing to observe and question our thoughts and stop subscribing to them blindly, then we have probably taken the most important step in our life. We can choose to stop engaging in repetitive and useless thoughts, rather entertain thoughts that are useful, uplifting, and creative. Most importantly, we begin to control our thoughts instead of allowing them to dictate us.

Practices

- Practise observing your thoughts. Sit in a comfortable place and try to observe your thoughts without judgment or labelling. Simply notice them as they pass by.

- Notice how thoughts effortlessly cross your mind. Even if you don't actively engage, thoughts continue to float effortlessly.

- Observe that when you don't invest much energy or attention in your thoughts, they come, linger for a while, and eventually dissipate on their own.

- Practise noticing things just as they are, without the need to label them. Whether it's a flower or a bird, focus on it without applying any labels.

- Practise these moments of thought-free awareness throughout the day.

- Using your sense of sight and hearing, explore your direct experience. When you see a tree, do you see it explicitly labelled as such, or is it your mind that immediately categorises it? When you hear a sound, does your mind label it as a car or a voice, or is it the sound itself that conveys what you're hearing? Keep an open mind during this experiment.

- Be mindful of thoughts, the space between thoughts, and the space surrounding thoughts.

- Determine whether you can distinguish between thoughts and awareness. Are they identical? Can there be awareness without thoughts?

- Subject any deeply ingrained beliefs to scrutiny. How would you feel if these beliefs were not true and merely narratives created by your mind?

- Compile a list of your limiting thoughts, the ones that induce feelings of separation, fear, and isolation.

- Is it true? Consider any thoughts related to a situation causing you anxiety or stress. Apply Byron Katie's method by asking yourself the four questions: Is it true? Are you certain it's true? How do you feel when you believe the thought? how do you feel when you let go of the thought?

8

GIFTS OF PRESENCE: AWE, WONDER, AND FLOW

'When it's over, I want to say: all my life
I was a bride married to amazement.
I was the bridegroom, taking the world in my arms.'
—Mary Oliver

It was a hectic day at work with numerous patients to examine and evaluate. The phone had been ringing incessantly since morning, and I was feeling a shade irritable and rattled. I finished seeing the patient on the fifth floor and checked my list to see which ward I had to visit next. There were constant calls from the OPD, informing me about the patients who were waiting for me.

As I turned, I paused to take a breath and looked down from the balcony of the ward. I could see the park below with people sitting leisurely and relaxing. It was midday in the month of February, and the sun felt warm and delicious against the cool breeze. The sight of the bright blue expansive sky and the sound of birds chirping was healing and lifted my heart a bit. For a moment, I forgot about everything else, became fully present, and simply savoured the whole experience.

The entire process took no more than a couple of minutes. It was a simple, ordinary moment, but it morphed into something beautiful and vibrant. In that moment of pausing and being present to what was happening, I was able to break the cycle of autopilot activity and hectic pace which was threatening to overwhelm me. And in the process of slowing down, I experienced a moment of awe and stillness, which felt deeply peaceful and liberating. I realised that even in the midst of the most frenetic activity, we could be free if we could remember to pause. The mundane could transform into a moment of awe and wonder.

Being mindful and present is not just about being aware of our anxious thoughts and emotions. It is also about being able to capture the exquisite joy and happiness of simply being alive.

When we are truly in the here and now, we can tap into an endless reservoir of awe and wonder all around us. What stops us from experiencing such periods of aliveness are our busy and hectic lifestyles, overwhelming thoughts, and ruminations. I can clearly remember a trip my family and I had made to London, which we had been looking forward to for months.

We were exploring the beautiful city of London on a glorious summer afternoon, but the weather inside me was a tad stormy, thanks to a disturbing phone call in the morning, followed by an argument with my wife. As a result, I was almost oblivious to all the beauty and charm around me, and nearly wasted the entire day lost in my thoughts. Even exotic locations or leisurely vacations don't guarantee bringing us to a state of awe and aliveness, while on the other hand, we don't really need to visit an exquisite destination to tap into beauty and wonder.

Awe

Awe can be described as a sense of aliveness, timelessness,

and expansiveness in the presence of something vast and profound. The term awe has mostly been reserved to describe the majestic beauty of wonders like the Taj Mahal or the Niagara Falls, but we can find such moments of awe almost anywhere when we are fully present.

Microdosing Mindfulness

Most of us are of the view that awe is a rare precious gift that we are treated to occasionally, while for a major part of our lives, we have to settle for the dreary and the mundane. However, that is not true.

Let me introduce you to a fascinating concept called 'Microdosing Mindfulness', which is a simple method of generating awe in our daily lives. We experience small moments of mindfulness several times a day, by using all our senses, becoming still, present, and noting the beauty all around us. How delightful our day can be if we are able to experience awe several times a day even in the most mundane activities like showering, cooking, or commuting.

Microdosing mindfulness involves pausing, fully taking in and appreciating what we are sensing—with our eyes, smell, and touch. As we become more present by learning to microdose mindfulness, we can experience awe while listening to music, cuddling our pet, or even in the midst of heavy traffic or hectic work.

The Greater Good Science Centre in the University of California, Berkeley, has been collaborating with Jake Eagle, author of *Power of Awe*, and his team regarding the scientific benefits of microdosing mindfulness. In their research, they found that patients who learnt to microdose mindfulness reported decreased chronic pain, reduced anxiety and depression, and noted greater happiness along with a sense of well-being.

According to researchers who study awe, including Michelle Shiota, Dacher Keltner, and Jonah Paquette, among others, two main conditions are needed to truly create a sense of awe. First, our encounter must be something vast, whether in the physical realm—such as a waterfall, sunset, or sky, which is known as perceptual vastness—or with an idea—like generosity, power, or greatness—which is known as conceptual vastness.

The second component of awe is that the experience transcends our understanding of the world, forcing us to change our assumptions and accommodate the new information. So, we can see that awe can be created from a wide repertoire of encounters. A breathtaking sunrise, a great act of valour or compassion, watching a poignant film, can all elicit a sense of awe. Awe may be in the form of life-altering and mind-blowing experiences like viewing the Grand Canyon, the Great Barrier Reef, or witnessing the birth of a newborn. Yet, as we have alluded to earlier, there is the everyday awe in noticing the changing colour of leaves, the soft breeze against our cheeks, or even a random act of kindness.

In his well-researched book, *Awestruck*, Jonah Paquette affirms that a key aspect of awe is that it enables us to feel a sense of connection to other people and to something larger than ourselves. Awe blurs the line between the self and the world around us, diminishes the ego and links us to the greater forces that surround us in the world and the larger universe. Not just that, it also motivates us to be kinder and more compassionate.

The Moral Beauty of Awe

In his book, *Awe: The New Science of Everyday Wonder and How It Can Transform Your Life*, Dacher Keltner talks about the moral beauty of awe, and how others are more likely to elicit a feeling of awe in us. It is about experiencing awe in the face of extreme courage, tender compassion, overwhelming odds, the underdogs, etc.

He suggests that acts of courage are a kind of moral beauty

with sublime potential, such as people using CPR to revive victims of cardiac arrests, parents raising children despite extreme adversity, bystanders going out of their way to help complete strangers. Compassion and kindness are other common examples of the moral beauty of awe, and so is overcoming obstacles, especially those who transcend mental and physical hurdles. After I read his book, I realised that the most fertile place to witness the moral beauty of awe was in a hospital setting—patients making miraculous recoveries, the sights of comatose patients waking up and recognising their kins, relatives and even strangers going out of the way to arrange for blood and medicines, the indefatigable and courageous doctors in the emergency room staying awake the entire night and dealing with critical patients. I remember having goosebumps when I saw my colleagues in the emergency and intensive care units battling it out during the COVID-19 pandemic. Moreover, we also experience awe when we see the underdogs rising against all odds.

Challenges in Experiencing Awe

The biggest obstacle to experiencing awe on a regular basis is our lifestyle. We are constantly on the move, shifting from one activity to another as if our lives depended on it, and are continuously glued to technology. While technology and social media are blessings in many ways, they prevent us from pausing, looking up, and connecting with nature and people. Our culture has been labelled as awe-deprived.

While travelling in a car or metro, we feel the need to keep our minds focused on either our phones or the FM radio playing music because we are unaccustomed to stillness and silence. Stillness is, in many ways, the mother of awe. It is only when we can pause that we notice the sacredness and beauty of ordinary things. Recent research on the emotion of awe, as compared to earlier times, focuses on the six major emotions—sadness, anger, fear, happiness, surprise, and disgust. Awe is no longer considered a luxury item of the mind. Dr Michelle Shiota, psychologist and awe researcher, states that: 'Awe is now coming to be seen as a crucial part of a meaningful life.' However, researchers are beginning to explore the timeless notion of awe with the help of modern science.

The most prominent benefits of awe:

a. Experiencing awe on a regular basis increases happiness and well-being, and individuals report higher levels of life satisfaction. U. C. Berkeley researchers have also found that these positive effects are not only short-term but can last for weeks.

b. Experiences of awe shift us away from mere materialism and align us with deeper, more meaningful values. This may lead to a shift toward a higher plane, connecting us to a larger world around us.

c. It reduces stress and anxiety.

d. It broadens our horizons.

e. It increases humility and a tendency towards less self-centred behaviour. A feeling of interconnectedness and interdependence is fostered.

Wonder

Wonder is a close relative of awe, and we often use the terms awe and wonder together. Author of the book *Tracking Wonder* and founder of the 'Tracking Wonder Consultancy', Jeffrey Davis, defines wonder as a heightened state of awareness brought on by something unexpected that delights or disorients us, or both. Goosebumps are the physiological response to a moment of wonder, and wonder can be found even in the most ordinary situations of life. In the book he discusses the six facets of wonder that often function in pairs:

1. The first pair is openness and curiosity. Openness is the wide sky facet that opens us to the possibility of finding wonder. Curiosity is a more proactive facet of wonder that questions and challenges the status quo of things.

2. The second pair is bewilderment and hope. Bewilderment is the disorienting facet of wonder when our sense of identity or even the ideas we are pursuing become confused. Hope is described as the rainbow facet, involving deliberate daydreaming and goal setting. These two facets are essential for building resilience and fortitude without burning out.

3. The third pair is connection and admiration. Connection speaks to our yearning to sync with one another, to connect with both strangers and friends. Admiration is a surprising love for someone else's excellence, character, or craft. Jeffery explains admiration as a kind of positive envy.

Through his research, Jeffrey points out that wonder is an excellent way to enhance the quality of our lives. He advises us to pause and ask ourselves questions from time to time to keep the wonder quotient alive in us. He particularly recommends that, at the end of the day, we ask ourselves what the highlight of the day was—this could be small moments like a great conversation or a token of appreciation given or received. Such wonder interventions can truly make our day memorable. It's common sense that we attract whatever we focus on in our lives. If our focus is on awe and wonder, we can transform even the most mundane times into magical, wonderful moments to be remembered.

The Role of Positive Emotions Like Awe and Wonder

What is the role of awe and wonder in our lives? Is it just about feeling good and pleasant, or do they have other long-lasting implications in our lives? Eminent scientist and researcher Barbara Fredrickson states in her book *Positivity* that emotions like awe and wonder have an impact even after the event that provoked them and have downstream consequences for the trajectory of our lives.

In her famous 'Broaden and Build' theory, she proposed that these positive emotions broaden our ideas about possible actions, opening our awareness to a wider range of thoughts and possibilities. Positive emotions like awe, wonder, and inspiration expand our hearts and minds, making us more receptive and creative. These emotions transform us for the better by allowing us to discover and build new ties, new knowledge, and new ways of being. This helps build resources for the future and new connections with people.

Another significant finding comes from the study of researcher Daniel Danner, who found that increased positivity helps increase longevity and survival. The good news about emotions like awe and wonder is that they can be cultivated, nurtured, and cherished through simple practices.

My Story of Awe and Wonder

It was the practice of mindfulness and being present that opened me up to the everyday world of awe and wonder. Earlier, feelings of awe and wonder seemed to arise a couple of times a year, mostly during vacations or breaks. Through mindfulness and awareness, I realised that we are all surrounded by moments of awe throughout the day.

We miss these precious moments because we are inundated by thoughts and overwhelmed by work. As a society, we have been brought up to worship work, busyness, and achievements, and trivialise or gloss over positive emotions. So, we lose the priceless connections in a heartfelt smile with a friend or even a stranger, the sensation of the wind against our cheeks, and the daily sunrise and sunset.

The best part is that mindfulness and positive emotions feed and amplify each other. The more aware and present we become, the more we notice what makes us feel this awe and wonder. The more we experience awe in our lives, the more mindful we become. I also strongly believe that having my heart fully exposed during my turbulent journey of helplessness and despair opened me completely and gave me access to a dimension that was earlier inaccessible. I became more aware of the exquisite beauty and awe all around me at a deeper level.

I understood completely what Kahlil Gibran meant when he said, 'The deeper that sorrow carves into your being, the more joy you can contain.' When we fully allow ourselves to feel sadness and pain, we can experience joy and beauty more profoundly as well.

Lose Your Mind; Come Back to the Senses

The simple secret to cultivating more awe and wonder in our lives is to come back to the senses. The more we tune in to our senses—hearing, seeing, touching, smelling, and tasting—the less we are lost in our thoughts and minds. Take a few minutes from your daily activities and come back to the sensations. Be aware of sights and sounds in your surroundings—the sound of the fan, people talking, dogs barking, birds singing, the sights and colours of nature, and the soft fragrance of flowers. This practice can help you escape from the tyranny of your thoughts and come back to the body and the present moment.

Small moments of awareness, even for a few seconds, repeatedly practiced throughout the day, will make this a simple habit to cultivate and cherish. As the famous German psychologist Fritz Perls said: 'Lose your mind and come to your senses.' Losing our minds and coming back to our senses is an antidote to our tortuous thoughts and ruminations. We stop obsessing about thoughts and come back to the present.

Flow

It was my wedding reception, and the guests were steadily arriving. The DJ was playing some great soundtracks, and my new wife and I were joyfully welcoming our friends and relatives. In the back of my mind, however, was the nagging thought that I had to leave home the next morning to appear for my MD practical viva exams, which were only three days away, in a different city. This MD practical exam was going to be one of the toughest exams in my career, given the small margin of error involved, and the fact that I had gotten married just before the exams due to unavoidable reasons. I experienced a fascinating cocktail of emotions like excitement, happiness, and fear all at once.

Suddenly, a friend came and said, 'Come, Saroj, let's dance the way we used to at our hostel parties.' I didn't need a second invitation. Leaving my surprised wife, I joined the dance floor and started dancing with full gusto. The DJ was playing all my favourite dance tracks, and I told myself that I had to make every second of these three or four hours count because, starting tomorrow, the next few days were going to be stressful.

I received a wonderful surprise when, after some time, my wife joined me on the dance floor, leaving the task of welcoming guests to our bewildered relatives. I was dancing with abandon and ecstasy, as if some energy and force were flooding into me from within and without. I don't remember eating anything either because I didn't want to cease that momentum.

Even though it's been 22 years since that day, and I have been to several events and live dance shows since, I can't recall anything more mesmerising than that night. It was only later when I was reading a book by the Hungarian-American psychologist Mihaly Csikszentmihalyi that I found a word that closely matched what I had experienced that night. It was called 'flow'.

In the Zone

We can describe flow as a deep immersion in an activity that causes you to lose track of time. There is an absence of time and space and even self. The above-mentioned example describes such a state, and I'm sure you will be able to recall a time in your life when you had the same experience. It can be while reading an enthralling book, being engaged in sports or music, dancing, or going on a holiday.

All categories of sportsmen, whether athletes, footballers, or cricketers, use the term 'being in the zone'. When Yuvraj Singh, the famous Indian cricketer, blasted Stuart Broad of the English team for six consecutive sixes in the T20 World Cup cricket in 2007, he described his state as being in total flow and in the zone. Things seem to happen spontaneously without much effort when we are in flow. It can be described as getting out of the way and letting some force take over.

There has been considerable interest in this topic because of its wide-ranging implications. Since I started practicing and teaching mindfulness, I became even more aware of and interested in it. Mindfulness is not the same as flow, but being mindful can be a primer for the state of flow, increasing the likelihood of *being* in the flow.

Mihaly Csikszentmihalyi discovered during his research on happiness that people were most creative, productive, and happy when they were in a state of flow. He interviewed athletes, musicians, and artists because he wanted to know when they experienced optimal performance levels. He was also interested in finding out how they felt during these experiences. Mihaly developed the term 'flow state' because many of the people he interviewed described their optimal states of performance as instances when their work simply flowed out of them without much effort.

He aimed to discover what piques creativity, especially in the workplace, and how creativity can lead to productivity.

He determined that flow is not only essential to a productive employee, but it is imperative for a contented one as well.

Csikszentmihalyi describes flow as, 'The state in which people are so involved in an activity that nothing else seems to matter; the experience itself is so enjoyable that people will do it even at great cost, for the sheer sake of doing it.'

Characteristics of Flow

Mihaly mentions these characteristics of flow:

- Complete concentration on the task
- Clarity of goals and reward in mind and immediate feedback
- Transformation of time (speeding up/slowing down)
- The experience is intrinsically rewarding
- Effortlessness and ease
- Balance between challenge and skills
- Actions and awareness are merged, going past self-conscious rumination
- There is a feeling of control over the task

The research on flow suggests that those with *autotelic* personalities tend to experience more flow. Such people tend to do things for their own sake rather than chasing some distant external goal. This type of personality is distinguished by certain meta-skills, such as high interest in life, persistence, and low self-centredness.

The state of flow has become a subject of intense research, and according to the neuroscientist Arne Dietrich, it has been associated with decreased activity in the prefrontal cortex. The prefrontal cortex is an area of the brain responsible for higher cognitive functions such as self-reflective consciousness, memory, temporal integration, and working memory. It's responsible for our conscious and explicit state of mind.

However, in a state of flow, this area is believed to temporarily downregulate in a process called transient hypofrontality. This temporary deactivation of the prefrontal area may trigger the feelings of distortion of time, loss of self-consciousness, and loss of the inner critic.

The balance of perceived challenges and skills are important factors in flow—as suggested by chess grandmaster Nakamura. When a challenge is bigger than one's level of skills, one becomes anxious and stressed. On the other hand, when the level of skill exceeds the size of the challenge, there is the risk of getting bored and distracted.

Flow Triggers

Steve Kotler, author of the *Art of the Impossible* and founder of the 'Flow Genome Project', has been researching about flow states for several years. He has identified more than twenty flow triggers that are most suited to inducing the flow state. All of them, according to him, work by driving attention into the present moment. Their mechanism is a combination of either pushing dopamine and/or noradrenaline into our system. They also lower cognitive load that frees up extra energy that can be then repurposed for attention.

Internal triggers—clear goals, immediate feedback, complete concentration, and the challenge-skill balance— are the most important. He lists the combination of attention and autonomy as both acting in tandem to trigger the flow state. The trinity of curiosity, passion-purpose ranks high among the intrinsic motivators that fuel flow. Flow follows focus, and when we are completely focused on the present moment, it becomes a portal to flow states. It follows that multitasking prevents such an engaged state from emerging.

His research also concluded that approximately 90 to 120 minutes of uninterrupted concentration was the ideal time period to maximise focus and flow. Steve also cites immediate feedback as opposed to delayed feedback as a shortcut to flow in combination with the other triggers. We have earlier alluded to the challenge-skills balance, which he lists as among the most important triggers. It is the sweet spot where the task is hard enough to make us stretch but not so tough as to make us snap.

In his book *The Rise of Superman*, Kotler arrives at a figure of four per cent as a magic number. According to him, if the challenge of that task is four per cent greater than our skill set, there is an increased chance of the task leading to a flow state. He gives his example of book writing and how he sets the daily word count to be approximately four to five per cent more than what he is comfortable with writing.

Steve also talks about the external triggers to achieve flow states. One of these is high consequences, which is about threats or fear lurking ahead. This resonated with me as I recalled my state of flow during the wedding reception, with the impending crucial exams giving that element of fear and threat to the excitement I was feeling about the party. The combination of novelty, unpredictability, and complexity can be a fertile ground. If we need to maximise flow in our lives, we need to create a similar environment around us. Steve suggests that nature offers high concentration of these three triggers and regular walks or occasionally working amidst nature can sometimes do wonders.

On the threshold between an external and internal environment sits deep embodiment. Deep embodiment is a type of expanded physical awareness. It means that we pay most attention to the task at hand when multiple senses are engaged in the task. Steve attributes this to the reason why sportsmen often get into the flow or zone state more than others. It is not surprising that creativity is another valuable flow trigger.

While flow is mostly referring to individual performances, there is a mounting interest on something called 'Group Flow'. Group flow refers to the shared, collective experience of a group of people performing at their peak. Group flow and team flow result from triggers that are innate in team dynamics. Here, again, complete concentration, focus, and shared, clear goals along with communication are imperative for group flow.

These results show us that flow is not exclusive to musicians and brilliant sportsmen but are ubiquitous. It shows up anywhere, in anyone, provided certain conditions are met. We simply need to be aware of the flow triggers and be willing to be open to the concept of flow.

The first step is to be aware of what flow is, how it can be achieved, and its benefits. The benefits of being in the flow state are manifold, including greater productivity and performance enhancement, improved happiness and well-being, and increased engagement. Researchers like Steve Kotler are helping in bringing about more flow into our daily lives so that our lives can be inspiring, creative, and enjoyable.

Often, we equate happiness and joy with achievements, or landmarks like birthdays and anniversaries, while we miss the subtle, lovely moments that are right in front of our eyes. We miss the beauty of the present moment because we are obsessed with the future, and in turn, we get lost in our thoughts. When we become more present and aware, we notice the exquisite aliveness and vibrancy of everything around us, and appreciate moments of awe, wonder, and flow right in front of us.

We can discover the small moments throughout the day that can brighten our hearts and make us feel the rapture of being alive. Begin by noticing what you are paying attention to because that makes all the difference. As author Julia Cameron beautifully explains, 'The quality of life is in proportion, always, to the capacity for delight. The capacity for delight is the gift of paying attention.' By altering our perspective on the world, we can transform even the most ordinary moments into miraculous experiences at any given time.

Practices

- Daily use the practice of microdosing mindfulness for a few minutes a day. Simply look at surroundings nearby and notice their stillness and beauty. Be present and notice your natural surroundings, the sunrise, sunset, or soft breeze.

- Take an 'awe walk' in any natural place in your vicinity and keep your senses open.

- How can you bring more awe in your life? Take pauses from time to time and notice things around you. It will increase your awe quotient.

- Make a list of things which bring you in flow—it can be music, dance, games, or reading.

- Try to incorporate something which brings you in flow in your daily routine. If it's dance, then shake a leg maybe three times a week. Make a conscious effort to incorporate it into your schedule even if it is for a short time.

- At the end of the day make a note of three things which filled you with wonder—a great conversation, a warm smile, or gesture. Make it a daily habit.

- Look at the changing landscape of the sky and clouds whenever possible and be present with it for a few seconds. That can bring you into a state of awe and wonder.

- At the end of the day recall a moment of genuine connection with someone, a genuine smile, or exchange of words, or just a warm 'Hi'.

- Try to bring a beginner's mind to situations as much as you can. As if you are seeing a tree, plant, or vehicle for the first time.

- Notice a child or a pet and how they view things with freshness, awe, and curiosity. When we observe their state of presence, we can come into stillness and presence, too.

- Tune into your senses. Whenever you get a few moments try to tune into your senses fully. Hearing, seeing, smelling, touching. Savour and linger on anything that feels good such as a tasty snack, or a nice view.

9

CREATIVITY: THE ART OF LIVING

'Creativity itself doesn't care at all about results—the only thing it craves is the process. Learn to love the process and let whatever happens next happen . . .'
—**Elizabeth Gilbert**

For a significant portion of my life, I believed that I lacked creativity. I could write a bit, was an avid reader, enjoyed sports and movies, but I was convinced that, since I couldn't draw or paint to save my life and was not adept at any musical instrument, I didn't possess a creative bone. I thought creativity was a privilege reserved for a select group of talented athletes or musicians, whose passion and profession aligned, and their rarefied existence had nothing in common with us ordinary individuals.

Furthermore, I always assumed that you were either born with creativity or not. It was only when I chanced to read the fascinating books *The Big Leap* and *The Genius Zone* by the celebrated author Gay Hendricks that I started to understand what creativity and passion truly meant and was inspired to find out more about them.

Zones of Activities

According to Gay Hendricks, our activities in the world broadly fall into four main zones:

1. The *zone of incompetence* consists of all the activities we are not good at but still have to do.
2. The *zone of competence* comprises of activities at which we may be fairly competent and efficient, but the same work could easily be handled by someone else.
3. The *zone of excellence* is what Hendricks describes as a seductive trap we often fall into. We may be talented and excel in this zone, possibly earning significant rewards, but this is not our real flow or special talent which is unique to us. He says that we should make the 'big leap' and dive deeper into the fourth zone of genius.
4. The *zone of genius* is the set of activities that we are uniquely suited to do. It draws upon our special gifts and strengths. It is innate to us, makes us thrive, and sees us at our creative best. He recommends that we should take initial baby steps in this direction, and gradually start increasing the time devoted to these activities by even 10 per cent. Once we start devoting more time to our passion, it creates the momentum for us to dedicate even more time and energy.

What Is Creativity?

Dr Danny Penman, a journalist and author of the book *Mindfulness for Creativity* describes creativity as the ability to perceive the world in new ways, to find hidden patterns, to make connections between seemingly unrelated phenomena and to generate solutions. According to him, creativity involves two processes: thinking and producing. Only having ideas without acting on them makes us imaginative but not creative.

No one elucidates creativity better than Elizabeth Gilbert, the author of *Eat, Pray, Love* and *Big Magic*. She explains that creative living isn't solely about dedicating a life devoted to arts, music, or poetry. It is about living a life that is strongly driven by curiosity than fear. According to her, a creative life is an amplified life, a bigger, happier, and more interesting life. More than anything else *we* need to have the courage to bring forth the jewels that are hidden within us.

Elizabeth has an interesting perspective on creative ideas, suggesting that ideas perpetually swirl around us, seeking available and willing partners. We only need to be open and relaxed and receptive enough to receive them. The idea will then orchestrate coincidences and omens to appear in our path, and we'll soon notice various signs pointing towards the idea. It's as if the idea is asking us, 'Do you want to work with me?' In a later section, I discuss how when we sit receptively in open awareness, inspiration and ideas will float in, seemingly out of the blue.

In her book *Big Magic*, Elizabeth provides an extraordinary description of how inspiration would strike the American poet Ruth Stone. Ruth had described to Elizabeth how, in her childhood, she could hear a poem rushing towards her, like a galloping horse. Ruth recognised this as a signal for her to rush back to the house, trying to reach a piece of paper and pen fast enough to quickly jot it down. There were moments when missed the poem and times when she would catch it just by the tail.

This is one of the most magnificent descriptions of how creativity and inspiration operate, throughout the ages, poets and scientists have recounted the serendipitous manner in which inspiration dawned upon them. It's as if we are simply channels for creativity and inspiration to manifest.

Why Is Creativity Important?

Austin Shaw Hill, a renowned creativity expert, founder of

'Creativity Matters', and author of *The Shoreline of Wonder*, explains the significance of creativity. In a 2010 IBM survey conducted amidst a global economic downturn, over 1500 CEOs from 33 industries and 60 countries reached a significant conclusion: 'More than rigour, management discipline, integrity, or even vision, successfully navigating an increasingly complex world will require creativity.' The study emphasised the need to instil creativity throughout organisations due to the challenges faced by CEOs in a rapidly changing environment.

Austin's life mission is to empower others as creators. He firmly believes that creativity transcends the boundaries between science and technology, art and business, religion, and spirituality, serving as a bridge that enables people from different disciplines, perspectives, belief systems, and ways of being to learn from one another. Moreover, he asserts that people find their greatest happiness and fulfilment in the state of creative flow. Ultimately, creativity possesses the power to heal by re-establishing a sense of wholeness, meaning, and intrinsic worth, leading to more skilful decision-making and serving the greater good.

In the book *Radical Brilliance* by Arjuna Ardagh, the author contends that our life's purpose should be to recognise our unique gifts and make a sincere effort to bring them to the world, giving them concrete form. Ardagh outlines the entire creative process, from the inception of an idea within us to its full flow, execution, and eventual dissolution. The four steps he outlines are—Awakening, Flow, Productivity, and Dissolution—making his book a recommended read for anyone aspiring to bring a creative dream to life.

Creative Thinking

Like Da Vinci, driven by my desire to delve into creativity and its mechanics, I delved into numerous books, including Michael J. Gelb's captivating work, *How to Think Like*

Leonardo da Vinci. Gelb not only explains how one can harness creativity but also emphasises that even if natural creativity isn't inherent, it can be cultivated with diligence and awareness.

Michael extensively studied the work and philosophy of the celebrated genius Leonardo da Vinci, distilling his teachings into seven outstanding principles. Leonardo da Vinci is widely acknowledged as one of the most exceptional geniuses in history, and Michael Gelb invested an extraordinary amount of time learning Italian and poring over Leonardo's handwritten notes to extract these principles.

The first principle he discusses is *curiosita* or curiosity. Leonardo possessed intense curiosity from childhood, which fuelled his genius throughout his life. Cultivating a 'beginner's mind' can help us become aware of the beauty and wonder around us.

Dimostrazione is the second principle, highlighting that experience is the source of wisdom. Leonardo continuously learnt, explored, and experimented, knowing that the experiences gained by attempting were valuable investments for the future.

Sensazione emphasises that our senses—sight, sound, touch, taste, and smell—are the keys to opening the doors of experience. Da Vinci believed that the secrets of *dimostrazione* were revealed through the senses, especially sight.

Sfumato is the fourth principle, encouraging openness in the face of uncertainty. Thriving amidst ambiguity and uncertainty is a potent strategy for unleashing creative potential.

Arte/Scienza is the fifth principle, advocating a balance of both right and left brain thinking. Leonardo was a creative genius and a brilliant scientist, believing that arts and science were inseparable.

The sixth principle, *corporalita*, highlights the importance of maintaining health and keeping the mind and body active and coordinated.

The final principle is *connessione*, emphasising the power of connecting disparate elements to create new patterns and recognising the interrelatedness of everything and everyone in a deeper sense. This principle aligns with recent advances in science and quantum mechanics, supporting the idea of interconnectedness in our world.

Creativity and Mindfulness

In his book *Mindfulness for Creativity*, Denny Penman explains that to enhance creativity, we need to cultivate three essential skills. Firstly, we require an open yet disciplined mind capable of gathering and integrating new ideas, concepts, and information, known as divergent thinking, occurring at both conscious and unconscious levels. Secondly, we need to consciously acknowledge the new ideas created by our minds and recognise their significance to prevent them from passing by unnoticed. Finally, we need the courage to pursue our ideas wherever they may lead.

The practice of mindfulness enhances divergent thinking, the purest form of creativity, which often conjures ideas seemingly out of nowhere. It is the state of awareness that led to Archimedes' Eureka moment, Isaac Newton's insights into gravity, and Einstein's theories, among many other strokes of genius. In short, it enables you to spontaneously find solutions, generate new ideas, and create insightful and creative works of art or design.

According to Denny, creative individuals tend to be more open and inquisitive, less constrained by existing categories and boundaries. They value exploration and curiosity as ends in themselves, love ideas for their own sake, and are willing to tinker with existing ones or use them as building blocks for new ideas. Creative people are not limited to writers and academics; they are also found in science, engineering, finance, and medicine. Denny Penman elaborates further on the two thinking styles associated with creativity.

Convergent Thinking

Convergent thinking is typically logical, rational, deductive, and focused. Its goal is to produce a single best answer to a problem with minimal ambiguity, emphasising speed, accuracy, and logic. It concentrates on recognising the familiar, employing established techniques, and accumulating stored information. Convergent thinking is most effective in situations where a readily available answer needs to be recalled or worked out. It emerges when the mind is in 'doing mode'.

Divergent Thinking

In contrast, divergent thinking is spontaneous and free-flowing, underpinning the purest form of creativity. It explores ideas through many possible solutions, often in parallel. Ideas may emerge suddenly as epiphanies or aha! moments. Divergent thinking involves exploring numerous potential solutions and drawing unexpected connections. It emerges when the mind is in 'being mode'.

Creative thought often combines both convergent and divergent thinking, each having its unique qualities. Studies show that mindfulness primarily boosts creativity by enhancing divergent thinking, although many qualities associated with convergent thinking are also improved by mindfulness.

According to researcher Ostafin, mindfulness enhances creativity by increasing intuition and insight while reducing cognitive rigidity, the tendency to make decisions based on habitual thought patterns, beliefs, and attitudes. Such cognitive rigidity can seriously hinder decision-making and limit creative thinking.

Doing vs Being Mode

Penman beautifully outlines the difference between the doing mode, which is characterised by convergent thinking, and the being mode, which is characterised by divergent thinking, in his book *Mindfulness for Creativity*.

1. Automatic pilot vs conscious choice: The doing mode efficiently automates our lives by creating habits but erodes creativity and openness. The being mode increases creativity by cultivating conscious awareness and mindfulness, encouraging us to move away from autopilot mode and embrace spontaneity.

2. Analysing vs sensing: The doing mode excels at analysis, thinking, planning, and comparison, but it can trap us in our thoughts. The being mode connects us more with our senses, being more intuitive, sensory, open-ended, and better at handling nuances and complexity.

3. Avoidance vs approaching: The doing mode clings to goals but also avoids threatening situations and has a narrow tunnel vision. The being mode embraces novelty, curiosity, and negativity.

4. Striving vs acceptance: The doing mode believes in effort and stress, while the being mode is characterised by relaxation and acceptance, creating without stress and anxiety.

5. Thoughts as solid and real vs thoughts as mental events: The doing mode obsesses over thoughts and ideas as its currency. The being mode recognises thoughts as passing mental events, understanding that they are real but not necessarily true.

The balance between both the doing mode and the being mode is essential for existence and creativity. Mindfulness helps restore the balance between them, teaching us to consciously switch between the two.

Eckhart Tolle, who emphasises the need for a balance between the doing mode and the being mode, spent two years in a state of joy and bliss after a profound awakening but found himself unable to function effectively in the world. He ultimately struck a balance between the two modes to be efficient, productive, creative, and happy.

It took me time to understand the implications of the being mode, as I had been a dedicated doer for most of my life. However, meditation and mindfulness practices opened new doors and insights, allowing me to tap into the being aspect. This enhanced my productivity, inner peace, grounding, and contentment, leading to the realisation that a balance between doing and being is necessary for wholehearted living.

The doing mode is powerful for solving problems but falls short when creative insights are required. To make creative leaps, we need to engage with the world through the being mode, referred to by neuroscientists as metacognitive awareness.

Barnet Bain, a Canadian film-maker and author, highlights the importance of falling in love with the dance of being and doing to become a skilled creator, merging will and action with imagination, feeling, and being.

Martin Aylward, a meditation teacher and author, believes that a sweet spot of focused relaxation, where attention is steady and open, leads to a flow state where creativity flourishes, whether in creativity, sports, or meditation.

Open Awareness and Creativity

Penman also posits that there is sufficient research to suggest that mindfulness meditation enhances the capabilities of divergent thinking and the being mode, thereby activating creativity. An important study by cognitive psychologist

Colzato compared the effects of focused attention to open monitoring meditation and concluded that focused awareness improves convergent thinking while open monitoring increases divergent thinking, aiding in insight solutions.

In the focused awareness method, we use the breath or senses as an anchor for mindfulness practice. In the open monitoring or open awareness method, we begin with using the breath as an anchor to bring calmness or focus, then gradually allow ourselves to be aware of all sounds, feelings, and sensations without labelling or judging them. We sit in awareness of all that appears without rejection or suppression, avoiding distraction by any thought or sensation. This way, we rest as awareness in awareness, providing fertile ground for ideas to emerge.

Let me share my limited experience. My preferred form of mindfulness practice is the open awareness method, as it is both relaxing and invigorating. When I initially decided to write this book, I felt apprehensive due to my lack of formal writing experience and uncertainty about having enough content for a book.

However, once the idea to write had taken root, I started the process. To my delight, sitting in open awareness with the intention of creating would flood me with ideas about chapters and topics, leaving me astounded. Patterns emerged seemingly out of nowhere, and new ideas surfaced. After my practice, I would jot down the ideas in a book to ensure I wouldn't forget them.

Get out of the Way

Frequently, we obstruct our true creative potential by being overly critical of our abilities and talent, believing we aren't sufficiently creative. We often become overly influenced by others' opinions and fear the comments or criticism we may receive. There's a negative inner voice that obsessively comments, and we must silence it.

Our most creative moments occur when we step aside and allow the source to guide us. We should fully support ourselves and trust the universe to facilitate the flow of magic through us. We need to surrender and let go, avoiding sabotaging our efforts with excessive anxiety about the final outcome. The best performance by a sportsman or artist occurs when they are willing to step aside, allowing for effortless manifestation.

Creative Thoughts

In his book *Radical Brilliance*, Arjuna Ardagh asserts that recycled thoughts are common. These thoughts are imitative, repetitive, borrowed from elsewhere and remembered. In many ways, they are repackaged and borrowed. The second kind of thought, the truly creative original thought, is rare. Ardagh labels recycled thoughts as horizontal, like small bubbles floating on the surface of a pond, each thought precipitated by a previous thought. Original thoughts, on the other hand, don't arise from the surface but from the depths. He calls them vertical thoughts, which start at the bottom and bubble to the surface.

Thoughts and ideas originating in this way begin as subtle impulses and become more vivid as they rise to the surface. These thoughts arise from the depths of our consciousness, and when we rest in open awareness, we can access those depths without striving.

According to Ardagh, striving and straining is the antithesis of accessing original or creative thoughts. He suggests that through practise, we can become more sensitive to subtle events in consciousness and harness these seeds of original brilliance and creativity.

We can start this creative process now by becoming more aware of the activities that bring us joy, aliveness, and happiness. We need to pause and ask ourselves, 'What makes me come alive and fills me with joy and fulfilment?' That is our 'zone of genius', our Ikigai, regardless of how small or significant the activity may be. It has always been dormant within us, silenced by the demands of daily life, responsibilities, and mundane chores.

We can learn to first recognise it, be mindful of it, and spend more time doing it. According to Hugh Delehanty, renowned author and mindfulness teacher, the key to creativity is about tapping into the resonance of the present moment. The goal is not to make art but to be in that wonderful state that makes art inevitable.

We must understand that when we use and share our creative gifts, it is not with the end goal of achieving bestseller status or hoping to strike gold. It is for the sheer joy of creating what we love. Brené Browne beautifully points out that creativity is not so much about what we do but who we are, and by not sharing it with the world, we do a disservice to ourselves. Elizabeth Gilbert's insight that in the process of creating we become a different person from when we started is the most significant reward of any creative pursuit.

Through my journey I've come to understand that we are all creative beings, and life is our canvas. We don't need to do anything specific to be creative—it can be the way we speak and reassure others, a heartfelt smile, words of appreciation, or an encouraging pat on the back for someone having a bad day. Each of us is uniquely creative and extraordinary, and we don't need to compete with each another. If we feel called to create something, we should not hesitate or hold back due to fear of adverse reactions and repercussions.

Barnet Bain's words resonate when he says, 'Our entire life is a freelance affair and the whole of life is a creative art. There is no act or thought or attitude that is uncreative. To live is to be creative.' Perhaps nothing can summarise this chapter more aptly than these soulful words by the writer Donna J. Stone: 'The most visible creators are those artists whose medium is life itself . . . They neither paint nor sculpt.

Their medium is being. Whatever their presence touches has increased life. They see, but don't have to draw . . .'

Practices

- Make a list of things that make you come alive—dancing, music, gardening?

- Begin a new hobby or passion today, something you have been contemplating for a long time but haven't started yet.

- Spend 15 to 20 minutes each day in open awareness, not doing anything, but simply sitting and allowing thoughts and ideas to visit.

- Start a journal to record new insights, questions, and contemplations. Note them down, no matter how small.

- Read about things purely for the joy of it, not to acquire knowledge or stay updated. Make it a habit to learn a new word or phrase. You may even learn a new language.

- Consider sharing your work if you are interested in languages or writing. If you are drawn to mindfulness, teach it to others, even for free. Let others know that you are willing to teach and see how it spreads.

- If you have the desire to draw, learn to draw or paint—don't worry about the results. Just splash colours and see how you feel. Practise playing with puzzles or riddles from time to time to keep your mind sharp. Learn to juggle.

- Recall a few occasions when you trusted your gut instincts to good effect. Trusting our intuition is also a practice, and we can start with trivial things.

- Try a different route to work, a different mode of transport from time to time, explore unknown terrains. All of these stimulate our creativity and keep the sense of wonder alive.

- Make a list of places where you get your best ideas from. Such as the shower, nature, or during meditation?

- Cultivate sfumato by taking time for solitude, for yourself, and by being open to whatever is taking place, embracing uncertainty.

- Start with small tasks, like mind mapping a vacation or an evening out.

- Reflect on whether you are predominantly right-brained or left-brained. If you lean towards the left brain, consider how you can incorporate more right-brain thinking into your life. If you are more right-brained, think about how you can develop more left-brain thinking.

- Use your non-dominant hand for writing, drawing, or tasks.

- Write or sign with your non-dominant hand.

- Learn to identify connections and patterns in your daily life. Can you draw connections between entirely unrelated things, such as a pen and an elephant, an athlete and a chess game, the global economy, and a mushroom?

- Create a list of 40 or 50 questions, such as: What is my life's purpose? How can I enhance my creativity?

10

HAPPINESS IS THE WAY

'There is a simple secret to being happy.
Just let go of your demand on this moment.'

—Adyashanti

Abhinav Bindra shot to instant fame and glory after winning the gold medal at the Beijing Olympics in 2008 for air rifle shooting. It was a historic and proud moment for Bindra and India because he became the first Indian ever to win an individual Olympic gold, and this was the pinnacle of his glory. It was a dream and passion that he had nurtured since childhood, and one can imagine how ecstatic he must have felt after finally achieving his dream, leading to unprecedented fame and success.

Many years later, Abhinav opened up about how he spiralled into depression soon after this moment of spectacular glory. He admits that although he had many ups and downs during his sports career, ironically his biggest mental crisis came after he achieved his greatest dream, an Olympic gold medal.

Bindra had nurtured the dream of winning an Olympic gold since childhood and dedicated 16 years of his life to training with singular focus, dedication, and perseverance. When he finally achieved this spectacular goal, he found that he had a large void in his life. He said in an interview with *The Indian Express*, 'One fine day, this dream, the goal was achieved but it created a very large void in my life. I think to me that was very challenging. I was depressed and was lost. I did not know what to do with my life and what to do next. That was probably the toughest moment of my life.'

He believes that we need to make a shift in our thinking and recognise that while there is a role for dreams and ambitions in life, we need to consciously make happiness our gold medal.

Isn't this a fabulous goal to seek? Most of us go through life as if it leads us by our nose. We see ourselves as puny beings pitted against a mighty force called 'life', with little power to eke sustained happiness. Life appears to be an ongoing struggle punctuated by moments of joy and success that sustain us. For the larger part, we swing between the pendulum of hope and fear.

For most of my life, I, too, subscribed to this world view because that was my family's attitude as well. I was taught that one had to study hard and get a respectable job, be successful at work, earn a decent salary, and have an understanding life partner. These were all the ingredients for happiness, and when I achieved all this, I thought I would be happy and at peace. After all, I had followed the perfect recipe for being truly happy.

However, life dealt me a huge blow through the Rashmi incident and woke me up from my slumber. It was only when I faced deep suffering and pain that I began to question the meaning of life and happiness. Was there a flaw in the recipe I was handed over by my elders, or was there something amiss with me? Perhaps I was doing something wrong and, therefore, unhappy?

These questions haunted me in the aftermath of the painful episode. It became my burning desire to probe deep into the reality of life and, at the same time, find the key to lasting happiness, meaning, and joy. I wanted to make *that* my gold medal. I intuitively knew that while my work as a doctor was definitely important, it was also imperative for me to find out the truth about life and happiness so that I could guide my children and others, too. I am not an expert, but my experiences and observations have been my teachers.

Over the last decade or so, the popularity of positive psychology has generated a lot of interest and research on the topic of happiness. One of the pioneers in this field is American author and orator Shawn Achor. Achor is one of the world's leading experts on human potential, with numerous research and publications on happiness and success. He designed the famous happiness course at Harvard and is the author of *The Happiness Advantage*.

In the book, he stipulates that most people around the world follow the formula of working hard to become successful. Once you do become successful, you will automatically find happiness. According to Achor, this formula is flawed and reads backward. There is enough groundbreaking research in the field of positive psychology and neuroscience to prove that the relationship between happiness and success is the other way around. Happiness is the precursor to success. Happiness and optimism fuel performance and achievement, giving us the competitive edge that Achor terms as the 'Happiness Advantage.'

He outlines seven principles in his book as the roadmap to a happier life:

1. The happiness advantage: We have been led to believe that happiness orbits around success, while there is enough research to prove that happiness is the centre, and success revolves around it. The most successful people don't look to happiness as some distant reward for their achievements. They capitalise on the positive and reap rewards at every turn. His

definition of happiness is the joy we feel striving after our potential. A study by Sonja Lyubomirsky, a professor of psychology at UC Riverside and the author of *The How of Happiness*, found that happiness leads to success in nearly every domain of our lives, including marriage, friendships, creativity, and career.

2. The fulcrum and the lever: Achor explains that by changing the fulcrum of our mindset and lengthening our lever of possibility, we can change what is possible. When we believe that we can bring about positive changes in our lives, it boosts our motivation and job performance.

3. The tetris effect: With practise, we can train our brains to scan for the positives and make use of the 'Happiness Advantage'.

4. Falling up: Once we are able to conceive failure as an opportunity for growth, we are more likely to experience that growth.

5. The zorro cycle: Limiting your focus to small, manageable goals can expand your sphere of power and help you achieve your most ambitious professional and personal goals.

6. The 20-second rule of habits: This is how one can turn bad habits into good ones by minimising barriers to change.

7. Social investment: In the middle of challenges and stress at work, there is nothing more crucial to our success than holding on to the people around us.

The Happiness Set Point

Many of us believe that we are born with our state of happiness, just like our complexion and height, and none of these can be changed much. We often meet people who seem to be perpetually discontented despite their achievements, wealth, and prosperity, while there are others who bounce back to their level of happiness even after facing enormously challenging circumstances.

Scientific studies prove that we are not completely wrong. Sonja Lyubomirsky, who has devoted her career to studying happiness, discovered that as much as 50 per cent of our happiness is derived from a genetically determined set point. This is an astounding number and is based on rigorous studies on identical and fraternal twins, followed over time. It is akin to our weight set point in many ways. Some are blessed with a skinny disposition while others, like me, have to struggle with weight all their lives.

While those with low happiness set points need to work a bit harder at their happiness levels. Those with high set points find it easier to bounce back to their previous states of happiness. However, we are wrong in concluding that we can do nothing about the situation.

Life circumstances, surprisingly, determine only 10 per cent of our happiness, claims Sonja. Whether we are rich or poor, married or divorced, beautiful or plain, affect our happiness levels only by 10 per cent. This is one of the greatest ironies of life. Most of our lives are dedicated to a mad quest to acquire more because of our conviction that more things will automatically make us happier.

Unfortunately, it will make us only 10 per cent happier. The reason for this miniscule increase is due to a powerful force in our life called Hedonic adaptation. Human beings are remarkably adept at adapting rapidly to sensory or physiological changes. Thus, we adapt to favourable changes in possessions, house, or wealth swiftly, and while it gives us a temporary dopamine high, it eventually plateaus down.

Can you remember the excitement you felt after purchasing a new car, a fancy house, or exotic furniture? How long did that euphoria last? I have been mindfully observing these feelings for a few years now, and I have found that the state of happiness post-acquisition lasts for not more than a couple of weeks, sometimes even less than that. After a couple of months, you may even need to be reminded about your new purchase.

This notion of 'I will be happy if . . .' or 'I will be happy when . . .' is one of the biggest fallacies of life. Wealth is a desirable commodity and can make our lives comfortable and enjoyable. It helps us remember the quote by the renowned architect Frank Lloyd Wright: 'Many wealthy people are little more than janitors of their possessions.'

Sonja explains in her book that one of the reasons for materialism's failure to make us happier is that when people attain their monetary targets, the achievement doesn't translate into happiness. I remember discussing this with a friend while holidaying together and relaxing over a couple of drinks. Both of us did our super specialisation in Gastroenterology from the same institute, and we were having this conversation about five years after graduation.

Getting this coveted degree was a dream for both of us, and now we were consultants earning a comfortable salary as compared to the pittance we earned during our graduation. He was complaining about the stress levels and reasons why things were not as smooth as we had envisaged, which led to his unhappiness. I pointed out that now that we had our dream job and were earning at least five times more, logically, our happiness should be—if not five times more—then at least double or triple.

If this was not the case, then it implied that our formula for happiness was somewhat faulty. If we simply continued along the same lines, we would not be much happier even after 15 years, though our income would have multiplied substantially by then. I decided that day to pursue what gave me happiness and joy, rather than blindly following what others were doing.

Happiness Activities and Strategies

If our happiness set point is largely genetic, and changing the circumstances of our life doesn't enhance our state of happiness too much, is it still possible to attain and sustain greater happiness? Sonja says that research provides positive and heartening news, and that the secret lies in the remaining 40 per cent of the pie chart. She says that if we observe genuinely happy people, we find they don't just sit around in contentment, but make things happen. They pursue new understandings and insights, seek new achievements, and monitor their thoughts and feelings. Thus, our intentional activities have a powerful effect on how happy we are, over and above the effects of our set points and life circumstances.

Sonja lists twelve activities that can increase our happiness quotient. While some practices may sound familiar, even corny, there is enough strong data to suggest that they can produce long-lasting results. These are:

- Expressing gratitude
- Cultivating optimism
- Avoiding overthinking and social comparison
- Practising acts of kindness
- Nurturing social relationships
- Developing coping mechanisms
- Learning to forgive
- Increasing flow experience
- Savouring life's joys
- Committing to your goals
- Practising spirituality and religion
- Taking care of your body

I was quite intrigued by Sonja's theory of Hedonic adaptation, and why gaining more in terms of fame and wealth may not always be the key to happiness. I found this to be borne out by the lives of many celebrities as well.

Famous Bollywood actress Deepika Padukone has been quite vocal about her battle with depression, which is a great example of the relationship between happiness, fame, and glory. She was at the peak of her career in 2013, giving four back-to-back hits and winning numerous awards. Her film, *Happy New Year*, had just been declared a blockbuster and one of the biggest grossers of 2014, and yet she was fighting a major battle with depression.

She has opened up about her challenging phase saying that waking up each day was a struggle. She would feel empty and sad and often break down privately. It was only when she confessed her feelings to her mother that the latter asked her to seek professional help. For Deepika, seeking help was the best thing she had done, for it helped her to come out of that phase. According to her, people simply could not fathom how she could be feeling unhappy, asking, 'How can you be feeling depressed? You have everything going for you.'

Deepika's poignant account highlights how we equate happiness with wealth, prosperity, and fame, and are unable to comprehend how superstars could possibly be unhappy despite the material comfort and reaching dizzying heights of fame. But when we look at the number of celebrities across the world who have ended their lives or have needed help, we can realise how temporary this kind of material happiness actually is.

Yet we continue to believe in the myth and encourage the younger generation to blindly chase after fame, success, and wealth, believing that attaining these goals are the key to happiness. I was discussing this with one of my close school friends, who was an exceptionally brilliant student and had been single-mindedly pursuing the dream of cracking the premier engineering exam of the country since childhood. Finally, when he secured a rank within the top 100 students, he was over the moon.

He later confessed to me that a few months after joining the institute, he went into depression because the reality was far from his expectations. In fact, he was so dejected that he went to the Himalayas for some time to search for the meaning of life, success, and happiness. He concluded that, as parents, we need to teach our children to make happiness and passion their most important goal, rather than cracking examinations or chasing degrees.

The Perma Model of Well-Being and Happiness

We will now discuss models of happiness endorsed by research. In developing a theory for well-being and happiness, Martin Seligman—the pioneer of Positive Psychology—selected five components that people pursue for intrinsic motivation and well-being. These elements are pursued for their own sake and are defined and measured independently.

These five components of the PERMA model comprise:

1. Positive emotions: More than mere 'happiness', including hope, interest, joy, love, awe, and compassion. Prime indicators of flourishing that can be cultivated for improved well-being.

2. Engagement: 'Being one with the music' in line with Csikszentmihalyi's concept of 'flow'. Much more powerful than simply 'being happy'; happiness is a by-product of engagement.

3. Relationships: Wholesome and healthy relationships are a powerful source of happiness. Research indicates that the quality of relationships determines longevity more than almost any other factor.

4. Meaning: The search for meaning and the need to have a sense of value and worth. Having a purpose in life helps individuals focus on what is important in the face of significant challenges.

5. Accomplishment: Also known as achievement, mastery, or competence. A sense of accomplishment is a result of working toward and reaching goals, mastering an endeavour, and having self-motivation to finish what is set out to do.

Role of Positive Emotions in Happiness

In chapter 8, we discussed the role of positive emotions in life and the research done by the eminent scientist Barbara Fredrickson in the field of awe and wonder. Her 'Broaden and build' theory focuses on 10 forms of positivity—joy, gratitude, serenity, interest, hope, pride, amusement, inspiration, awe, and love.

Positive emotions open and expand our outlook, making possibilities unfold. Positivity broadens our mind and expands our vision, leading to a 'broaden effect'. It is an especially good investment when creative solutions are needed fast. Positivity helps in coping with adversity, generating solutions, and triggers an upward spiral leading to growth and interconnectedness.

Pillars of Well-Being

Richard Davidson, a renowned neuroscientist and psychologist, identified four pillars for well-being:

1. Awareness: Cultivated through practices like meditation and mindfulness, attention is crucial for well-being.

2. Connection: Compassion and generosity are essential tools for well-being.

3. Insight: Understanding the narratives of the mind helps transcend its drives.

4. Purpose: Finding meaning and purpose in life contributes to overall well-being.

The Practice of Savouring and Taking in the Good

Among the various practices to enhance happiness, 'savouring' and 'taking in the good' are personal favourites. Effective in personal experience and backed by scientific research, savouring is the process of lingering on a positive moment with the intention of prolonging the feeling.

Savouring the small, good moments daily helps improve overall well-being. 'Taking in the good experiences' involves consciously soaking in pleasant experiences, contributing to neuroplasticity and the development of new neurons. Neuropsychologist Rick Hanson has worked extensively on his credible theory, which suggests that human brains have developed an evolutionary 'negativity bias', being like Velcro for bad experiences and Teflon for good news. We can reverse this bias by deliberately absorbing the pleasant experiences we encounter every day instead of letting them slide.

Happiness Is Our True Nature

Many of the doubts I had about happiness, joy and peace were clarified by eminent spiritual teacher and author Rupert Spira in his invaluable book *You Are the Happiness You Seek*. Rupert suggests that the exploration of happiness has been at the centre of man's existence since centuries. He categorically states that happiness is not to be found in any objective experience; both happiness and joy are our innate nature. For instance, a person wanting a new car is overjoyed when they finally buy it, while someone else who desires more money becomes ecstatic when they win a handsome lottery prize. A third person dreaming of a romantic relationship feels blissful when they meet their soulmate.

In all the above-mentioned cases, the objective experience is different, but the end result is the same—happiness. This gives us a clue that something is common to the experiences of happiness. Whatever the object of happiness may be, the experience of happiness is the same for all. Rupert further explains that happiness arises when the agitation of the mind subsides after the object is possessed, and once the agitation of the mind is alleviated, our true nature shines forth as happiness, joy, and peace. Therefore, it is not in the outward object that happiness lies, rather it is our very being whose nature is happiness. Our true nature has been given numerous names, such as beingness, awareness, self, or consciousness.

If happiness lay in an object like money, job, or relationship, it would be logical to expect these objects to induce the same level of happiness in everyone, which is not the case. Rupert explains that happiness may be indirectly experienced by acquisition of the object, because that allows our inner nature to shine forth as causeless joy and happiness. Then why not, he asks, make discovering our inner nature the ultimate goal. There is not a single path to happiness but Rupert dives straight into the heart of happiness and invites us to go directly to the source rather than around it.

Happiness Is in the Present Moment

We are often so focused on the future that we miss the present moment. The next job, the anticipated holiday, or a new relationship, we always seem to have our goals set on a distant future. We think we will be truly happy once the goal is achieved. According to Eckhart Tolle, the secret to happiness is surrendering to the present moment, saying 'yes' to what is happening in the moment. Whenever we are unhappy or stressed, it means that we are not aligned to the present moment and are trying to escape from the now. We may justify ourselves by saying that often the present moment is stressful or boring or even, at times, unbearable. So, how is it possible to stay in the present moment?

Eckhart mentions that we must make a distinction between the content of the present moment and the present moment itself, which is deeper than form. The content is ever-changing and temporary, one moment is unbearable, and the next moment is enjoyable. The content is conditioned by our thoughts, beliefs, and preconceived notions about how we may want the moment to be. However, by accepting the suchness of this moment, we allow this moment to be as is. There is no struggle or resistance. When we stop resisting, we experience a sense of stillness and spaciousness, which is quite joyful and peaceful. We connect with a dimension of alert presence, which is peaceful and spacious, still and alert. This, says Eckhart, is real happiness. Not the happiness that is at the mercy of external circumstances but happiness that can never leave us, because it is our very essence, our true nature.

Happiness Without a Reason

Tara Brach, spiritual teacher and author of *Radical Acceptance*, also dives into the topic of happiness. She explains that for most of us there are two kinds of happiness, the more common of which is happiness derived from obtaining certain objects, which she labels as happiness for a reason, and the second is happiness without a reason. Tara suggests that a lot of us feel our happiness is subject to fulfilment of certain conditions that may be lacking at this moment, thus, rendering us unhappy.

As a result, we postpone happiness in the belief that 'if only' this person would change or that object were acquired would we be truly happy. Or we believe that things 'should have' been like that or not like this. Our lives are suspended between the 'if only' and the 'should haves'. Tara explains that we don't really need a particular reason to be happy when we are in touch with our beingness. In this state of presence, even the smallest things can bring joy to our hearts as long as we are open and receptive. She advises us to be curious about the moments we feel alive and joyful and explore how it is our state of beingness and presence that is the cause of our happiness and not the object or situation.

Gail Brenner, author of *The End of Self-Help*, points out that the belief that happiness is in the remote future and we have to struggle to achieve it, is ingrained in us. She says that the great news is, the peace and happiness that we yearn for is available in this instant. When we realise there is unlimited potential for happiness right at this moment, it can bring a radical shift in our thinking.

Practices Leading to True Happiness

Below is a list of practices that I have personally found most fulfilling that lead to true happiness.

1. Say Yes/Acceptance: If I must cite one factor that has made a major difference in my life, it is 'acceptance' and saying 'Yes' to what is. This is not an exaggerated positivity but a quiet acceptance of whatever is taking place at the moment. The situation may not be the way I envisaged it to be or want it to happen, but I have to accept the *is-ness* of the moment. During challenging times when things are not going the way I would like them to, I whisper to myself 'Say yes', which helps me to surrender to what is taking place. There is this trust in the flow and intelligence of life, an innate belief that life always knows what is best for me and I have to go with its flow.

2. Space: An arising of spaciousness is an important component of happiness for me. I have discovered over the years that there has been an increase in inner space as well as space between my thoughts

and emotions, for which I would give credit to the practice of meditation, mindfulness, and periods of simply sitting in silence. I find myself responding to situations more often than reacting to them, as I would earlier. There has also been a growing understanding over time that my true nature, beingness, and this encompassing space of awareness are not different in any way.

3. Presence: I have faced periods of unhappiness whenever I have lost alignment with the present moment. It may be either being lost in thoughts, feeling overwhelmed with stress, or resisting the present moment and believing that it is not enough. A useful mantra for me over the years has been to ask myself 'Am I resisting this moment?' and if I am not aligned with the now, this question gently brings me back to the present.

4. Engagement/Flow: Engagement or Flow is an important part of happiness in my experience. Being in the flow and fully engaged in what I am doing is a surefire recipe for joy and happiness. It may be the work I am doing, reading, teaching mindfulness, or even dancing. The form of engagement keeps on varying, but the by-product of happiness is the same. Each one of us can become aware of what engages us or gets us in the flow and try to cultivate more of that activity into our lives.

5. Positive Emotions: Cultivating positive emotions has a vital bearing on our day-to-day happiness. Feelings of awe, wonder, compassion, and gratitude make life joyful and inspiring. The more we tap into awe and gratitude, the more reasons we can find to be grateful for.

6. Habits: Over the years I have found that nurturing certain habits play an important role in bringing joy

and fulfilment. Whether it is the habit of mindfulness or meditation or cultivating positive emotions, they all have a deep effect on my well-being.

In conclusion, the pursuit of happiness involves aligning ourselves with the symphony of life rather than the instruments that bring it about. By loving what is and accepting the present moment, we allow the music of life to permeate us with happiness and joy.

Practices

- Make a list of the activities that bring you happiness and reflect on how much time you are devoting to them.

- Reflect on a holiday and the thrill and joy of viewing the beautiful scenery. Introspect whether this happiness and joy lie in the scenery (object) or if they come from within when the mind's activity has subsided a bit.

- Think of the last time you bought something new and notice how long that happiness lasted. The next time you buy a new object, e.g., a car, furniture, stay aware of how long the novelty lasts.

- Make a list of three things to be grateful for every day. Reflect on moments of great happiness and success in your life, such as getting admission into college or landing a coveted job. Also, recall your burning desire to attain them. Reflect on whether the happiness is due to the subsiding of your desire, which was a source of agitation, or about acquiring what you wanted. Be still when you ponder about this; take some time to reflect on it.

- Do you equate success with happiness? Do you feel success automatically brings happiness? Observe your thoughts.

- How do you think money is related to happiness? Is there always a proportionate increase, or do you find that beyond a point money's ability to induce happiness reduces?

- Do you often talk about happiness with your spouse, friends? Do you read books or listen to talks on happiness? You may start a practice of journalling your views or thoughts.

- Are you convinced that happiness is an outside job, or do you believe it comes from within?

- Start a practice of savouring what brings you joy, such as a meal, scenery, or a nice conversation with a loved one.

- Make a practice of deliberately taking in the good. Enhance any good experience you had, such as a compliment or a gesture. Absorb it and hold on to it a bit longer than you otherwise would.

- Notice the background of peace when you are happy. Be aware that the background of stillness is always there.

- Notice the effect of positive emotions. How do you feel when you experience awe, joy, or optimism? Do you feel expanded or contracted? Does your vision become narrow or does it broaden?

- How can you cultivate more positive emotions in your life?

- Practise mindfulness and spend five minutes in silence every day.

- Ask yourself what is hindering your path to happiness?
- When faced with challenges, gently tell yourself, 'Say Yes.' Accept what is happening without resistance.
- Take a moment to check within and see if you are happy and at peace. Is there something lacking at this moment? This is not about the content of your life but life itself. Can you be happy right now without being overshadowed by the stories of your life?

11

EMBRACING KINDNESS AND SELF-COMPASSION

'People aren't longing to be impressed; they're longing to feel like they're home. If you create a space full of love and character and creativity and soul, they'll take off their shoes and curl up with gratitude and rest, no matter how small, no matter how undone, no matter how odd.'

—Shauna Niequist

The train crashed into the station, injuring hundreds, including the critically hurt engineer. Amidst the chaos, a woman was pinned under fallen station debris, fearing for her life. Fellow passengers formed a human chain, saving her. Unable to identify her rescuers, the woman compiled a list of those present that day. Despite asking each one if they helped her, they all denied it. Determined to express gratitude, she started helping them in various ways, like unpacking groceries and assisting a widower. This cycle of kindness continued for weeks. Eventually, she realised that not knowing her direct helpers allowed her to extend gratitude and aid to everyone she met—a divine symmetry of kindness.

175

This excerpt, taken (and rewritten) from Mark Nepo's book *Things That Join the Sea and the Sky: Field Notes on Living*, delivers a heartwarming message in these turbulent times. In life's journey, we have been offered a helping hand by so many people in various ways that it is difficult to repay everyone. But the lesson from 'The Symmetry of Kindness' is that it is our duty to offer help and compassion to whoever we find in need. This process starts a cycle of kindness.

This is exactly the mission of Orly Wahba, founder of the nonprofit organisation 'Life Vest Inside' and author of *Kindness Boomerang*. According to Wahba, our life vest, our ability to overcome hardships, to make it through, comes from 'inside'. Through the kindness we bestow on others and through the kindness others bestow upon us, we help keep each other afloat in the stormy seas of life.

She explains that though we can't prevent life's obstacles and challenges from coming our way, we can certainly throw someone a life vest, a lifeline of kindness. She mentions that one of the first things she did as CEO of Life Vest Inside was to make the video 'Kindness Boomerang', which shows how one act of kindness inspires another, and finally comes full circle.

When I watched this beautiful video with the song 'One Day' in the background, I had tears in my eyes, and the entire day I was searching for opportunities to shower acts of kindness. Make no mistake, kindness can save lives.

I read a touching story some time ago, where a young unemployed person was so disheartened with his life that he set out to commit suicide. He changed his mind at the last minute when a stranger spoke to him compassionately and encouragingly. Convinced there was still some hope in the world, the man decided to live a little longer. The next day he got an appointment letter for a job which he had applied for some months earlier but had lost hope and forgotten about. This was the starting point of a new life with hope and possibilities for the future.

Once he stabilised himself, he began searching frantically for the stranger who saved his life simply by a word of compassion but could not find him anywhere. Doubtless, he too must have lent a compassionate hand to others he encountered who were in despair.

The Rabbit Effect

Dr Kelli Harding, a medical psychiatrist, passionately advocates kindness and connection for leading happier, healthier lives. Her book, *The Rabbit Effect*, beautifully reveals the link between longevity, happiness, and health with the groundbreaking science of kindness.

Dr Harding came across a 1978 study with Dr Robert Nerem and his team, researching the effect of diet on rabbit hearts. A group of rabbits, inadvertently petted and talked to, performed significantly better, surprising everyone with their healthier hearts.

This unplanned finding intrigued Dr Kelli, leading her to explore the impact of kindness and social connections on health. To her delight, robust data suggested that apart from diet, exercise, sleep, and medicines, relationships significantly contribute to health. Dr Kelli's life and career revolved around: 'What are we missing in medicine?' 'Does the way we treat each other impact our heath?'

She emphasises that while it is imperative to invest on the latest technology, community-based low-cost interventions like hugging, chatting with friends, smiling at strangers can have a long-lasting effect. Recent research indicates that love, friendship, community, life's purpose, and environment can influence health more than doctors' office visits.

From a medical standpoint, I resonate strongly with Dr Kelli's hypothesis. As observed in practice, patients often defy medical odds, recovering unexpectedly, or conversely, suffering significantly despite seemingly minor illnesses.

Mindset, immunity, positive thinking, and interpersonal interactions all play roles in health outcomes.

I have lost count of the number of times my patients comment on how my warm smile or reassuring words have done more for them than all the medicines prescribed to them. While earlier I would simply brush these compliments aside as casual chit-chat, I no longer take them lightly and believe that the treating doctor's words and gestures can have a huge impact on patients' health.

The Kindness Test Project

Kindness has evolved from being regarded as noble but of little practical value to becoming a subject of extensive research and curiosity. The Kindness Test Project conducted on 60,000 people in 2021 by researchers from Sussex Centre for Research on Kindness, aimed to explore the relationship between kindness and health and well-being. The questionnaire was designed to study how kindness is viewed within society, with questions such as:

- What are the most common kind acts people carry out?
- Where do people most often experience kindness?
- What are the barriers to behaving kindly?
- How is kindness valued in the workplace?
- What prevents people from being kinder?

The results, published in March '22 on the 'Anatomy of Kindness' radio programme, revealed a link between kindness and well-being. Individuals who gave, received, or noticed more acts of kindness reported higher levels of well-being. Locations such as home, medical settings, workplace, and shops were identified as places where acts of kindness were more likely to be observed. Key barriers to kindness included concerns about misinterpretation (65.9 per cent), lack of time (57.5 per cent), and the perception of kindness as a weakness (27.5 per cent). Notably, the study observed that people were more likely to receive help if they asked for it.

This landmark study scientifically affirms what many have believed to be true—kindness is more prevalent than assumed. The pandemic has highlighted the hidden potential of kindness on a large scale.

Wired for Compassion

Studies on infants, children, and animals suggest our innate wiring for kindness and compassion, not something artificially created. Life's circumstances and conditioning veil our innate ability for love, connection, and compassion. Kindness benefits the doer more than the recipient, creating a 'kindness high' even from small acts.

Asking for help is a rewarding act, as it creates a positive cycle of kindness. It may seem counterintuitive, but asking for help brings joy and a sense of achievement. Inspired by Ben Franklin, who emphasised the inherent rewards of kindness, I occasionally ask for small acts of kindness.

Observing the two-fold blessing of kindness, as stated by Franklin and Shakespeare, reinforces the idea that kindness benefits both the giver and receiver.

Mindfulness is crucial for kindness and compassion. Being mindful and present allows us to notice others' feelings, expressions, and unspoken sadness. Pausing and listening enhance awareness, enabling us to notice more.

Conversely, stress and haste hinder compassion and empathy. Reflecting on a day after a talk about kindness, I intended to be kind but, overwhelmed by workload, lost patience and snapped at the nursing staff. Recognising this, I chose self-compassion over self-castigation, acknowledging its equal importance in our overall well-being.

Kindness and the Happiness Track

Author Emma Seppala delves into kindness as a crucial means of cultivating happiness in her book *The Happiness Track*, supported by substantial data. She explains that it is mainly the economists who have promoted the idea of self-centredness for happiness. She suggests that the notion of survival of the fittest is often misattributed to Charles Darwin, while it was actually coined by a political theorist, Herbert Spencer.

Darwin, by contrast, argued that 'communities which included the greatest number of sympathetic members would flourish best and rear the greatest number of offspring.' Emma argues that compassion and kindness are the actual cause of our survival over the centuries. What Darwin called 'sympathy' would today be termed as empathy, altruism, or compassion, according to psychologist Paul Ekman. We don't need to go any further than the COVID-19 pandemic, which showcased stories of courage, compassion, and connection, from medical staff to strangers risking their lives for one another.

My wife demonstrated such bravery during the pandemic. In the harsh phase of Covid in New Delhi, I, too, contracted the virus. My wife received a frantic call from her friend, seeking help for her husband whose health was rapidly deteriorating. As I was in isolation and couldn't help much, however, despite the risks and challenges, my wife promptly decided to accompany them for a CT scan and later arranged for the husband's hospital admission, showing tremendous courage and compassion.

Emma Seppala explains the medical reasons behind the empowering nature of compassion and kindness. When our brains shift from self-focus and stress to caring and connecting, it slows down our heart rate, activates the vagal tone and parasympathetic system, in turn, calming and nourishing the body. This not only enhances compassion towards others but also fosters a deeper sense of personal nurturance and positivity.

She quotes data to suggest that charitable activities and simple acts of kindness have equally beneficial effects on both givers and receivers. Data suggests that compassion is advantageous for health, with positive relationships associated with 50 per cent increased likelihood of longevity, reduced stress, a strengthened immune system, and lower rates of anxiety and depression.

Compassion and Success

Compassion's relationship with success, particularly in the workplace, challenges the perception that compassion is a soft skill incompatible with success. Kim Cameron and colleagues at the University of Michigan found that compassionate practices in organisations significantly improved performance levels, enhancing organisational effectiveness, including financial performance, productivity, and customer satisfaction.

In the workplace, a compassionate culture not only boosts employee well-being and productivity but also improves client health outcomes and satisfaction, as confirmed by a substantial healthcare study. Christopher Kukk, author of *The Compassionate Achiever*, argues that compassion builds successful businesses, governments, schools, and civic communities. Companies like General Mills, Aetna, Target, and Google have incorporated compassion into their structures, resulting in increased productivity and employee satisfaction.

Research by Barsade et al. published in the *Administrative Science Quarterly* reveals a positive correlation between compassionate behaviour, work satisfaction, and company success. Kukk introduces a four-step programme for cultivating compassion, condensed into the acronym LUCA: Listening, Understanding, Connecting, and Acting.

Compassion: Canulation of the Heart

Compassion is not merely a sentimental, wishy-washy feeling; it requires courage and an acceptance of one's vulnerability. As beautifully explained by Pema Chödrön in *The Places that Scare You*, cultivating compassion involves drawing from the entirety of our experience—our suffering, empathy, cruelty, and terror. Chödrön emphasises that compassion isn't a hierarchical relationship between a healer and the wounded; it is a connection between equals. True compassion emerges when we fully understand our own darkness and, in turn, can be present with the darkness in others, acknowledging our shared humanity.

Chodron's insights resonated deeply with me. Only after surrendering to and embracing my own darkness and suffering could I authentically empathise with others. This process opened my heart to a profound sense of shared humanity. I now find myself experiencing compassion and a sense of connection with complete strangers, recognising the interconnectedness of us all.

While the demands of a busy schedule can trigger impatience, especially with patients, being present and open brings a deeper joy in connecting with them. Despite differing opinions, a profound bonding at a deeper level is possible. I am genuinely curious about the lives of those I encounter, finding inspiration in how individuals, such as drivers, domestic helps, or watchmen, navigate significant challenges with a smile. Even when unable to offer tangible help, the act of listening is appreciated. I previously mentioned the medical procedure ERCP, a part of my professional expertise, but I find greater satisfaction in metaphorically cannulating the hearts of people with compassion, whether they are patients or those I interact with.

Achieving this compassionate connection brings immense happiness and fulfilment. Wendy Mass' words resonate with me, 'Be kind, for everyone you meet is fighting a battle you know nothing about.' Recognising that each person is grappling with something underscores the importance of kindness. According to Brené Brown, the core of compassion is acceptance, and the more we accept ourselves, the better equipped we are to show compassion to others.

Mark Nepo poignantly describes the common thread of being that transcends our differences. Each of us is born with a filament of being, fostering a spiritual pollination that connects us all. Despite our diverse experiences, this shared spiritual pollination is the source of a renaissance of care that blossoms in every generation.

Self-Compassion

Having explored the virtues of compassion towards others, we now turn to an equally, if not more, important aspect of kindness—self-compassion. We often find it relatively easy to be compassionate towards others, however, showing the same kindness to oneself can be challenging. Often, we set high demands, criticise ourselves for perceived shortcomings, and harbour harsh judgments.

Psychologist and author Dr Kristin Neff observes that the relentless pursuit of high self-esteem has become a tyrannical virtual religion in our competitive culture. The expectation to be exceptional and special leads to an unstable sense of self-worth, dependent on achievements and failures. Dr Neff advocates for an alternative path to happiness, which is self-compassion. Research suggests that individuals with higher self-compassion lead healthier, more productive lives than those who are self-critical.

In simple terms, self-compassion involves treating oneself with the same kindness and care extended to a friend. It requires accepting oneself with an open heart. Dr Neff emphasises that compassion should not be limited to others but should begin with self-compassion. Contrary to the belief that self-criticism motivates, it often results in anxiety, feelings of incompetence, and depression. Self-compassion, as revealed by Dr Neff's research, enables a clear self-perception and facilitates positive changes motivated by self-care.

Acknowledging our own needs for love, acceptance, and security, Dr Neff suggests that self-compassion can provide these feelings independently. This approach allows us to have more to offer to others from a place of genuine care. Dr Neff's research indicates that self-compassion yields the same benefits as high self-esteem without the drawbacks of self-righteousness, prejudice, or narcissism.

Embracing self-compassion frees us from the pursuit of perfection, opening the door to genuine happiness and satisfaction. It eliminates the self-condemning process of constantly comparing ourselves to others and questioning our worthiness. The three main components of self-compassion, as defined by Dr Neff, are as follows:

1. Self-kindness vs self-judgment

    Self-compassion entails being warm and understanding towards ourselves when we suffer, fail, or feel inadequate, rather than ignoring our pain or criticising ourselves. Self-compassionate people recognise that being imperfect, failing, and experiencing life difficulties is inevitable, so they tend to be gentle with themselves when confronted with painful experiences.

2. Common humanity vs isolation

    Frustration at not having things exactly as we want is often accompanied by an irrational but pervasive sense of isolation—as if 'I' were the only person suffering or making mistakes. However, the very definition of being 'human' means that one is mortal, vulnerable, and imperfect. Therefore, self-compassion involves recognising that suffering and personal inadequacy are parts of the shared human experience.

3. Mindfulness vs over-identification

Dr Neff suggests that self-compassion also requires taking a balanced approach to our negative emotions so that feelings are neither suppressed nor exaggerated. It also stems from the willingness to observe our negative thoughts and emotions with openness and clarity, so that they are held in mindful awareness.

I firmly believe that as medical professionals and caregivers, we particularly need to administer ourselves a healthy dose of self-compassion. While maintaining high standards of care, the challenging working environment, long hours, stress, and demanding nature of patients and their relatives can take a toll. The rise in medical litigation adds another layer of pressure, especially for interventionalists who often navigate precarious situations. When outcomes deviate from expectations, there is a tendency to self-blame, questioning if different actions might have yielded a different result.

A poignant lesson in self-compassion unfolded during my experience with Rashmi. In the aftermath of a complication and the subsequent weeks on life support, I found myself replaying the procedure in my mind numerous times. Despite knowing there was no flaw in my technique, I took full blame for the unforeseen outcome. Mindfulness training played a crucial role in my healing process, allowing me to extend the compassion and kindness needed. While the consequences were tragic, accepting that I wasn't to blame empowered me to heal and forgive myself.

It is vital to recognise that self-compassion for a doctor doesn't equate to negligence or carelessness. Instead, it involves understanding that, beyond offering our best expertise and knowledge, some factors are beyond our control. Medical professionals and caregivers who extend kindness and compassion to themselves are better equipped to serve their patients. Dr Neff's research suggests that continuous giving without self-care increases the risk of burnout and stress for caregivers, both medical and non-medical. Studies indicate that self-compassion is an effective way to enhance well-being and reduce burnout among healthcare professionals.

Shame and Self-Compassion

Closely linked to self-criticism is the emotion of shame. Brené Brown, an expert researcher on shame and vulnerability, defines shame as the gremlin that tells us we are not good enough, shouldn't have done something, or don't deserve something. Shame is a profoundly painful feeling of believing that we are flawed and unworthy of love and belonging. It keeps us small, resentful, and afraid, hindering innovation and creativity. Brown emphasises the need to cultivate awareness about shame, speak about it, and dismantle its power.

According to Chris Germer, shame may often be concealed beneath anxiety or anger, requiring a deeper exploration. Guilt and shame differ, with guilt focusing on a specific action while shame convinces us that we are inherently bad. The antidote to shame, as Germer suggests, is self-compassion. This caring attitude acts as a healing balm for the wounds of shame, fostering connection, empathy, and resilience. Brown terms this process of applying self-compassion to shame as shame resilience, outlining its elements in her work.

In *When Things Fall Apart*, Pema Chödrön explains that compassionate action involves working with ourselves as well as others. It requires staying open to our feelings instead of shutting down and pushing them away. Self-compassion entails accepting every aspect of ourselves, even the parts we dislike, demanding courage and openness. In an open, non-judgmental space, we acknowledge our feelings, even the unpleasant ones. Pema emphasises that compassion starts and ends with having compassion for all the unwanted parts of ourselves, including the imperfections we avoid acknowledging. Understanding that what we dislike in ourselves, we'll dislike in others, deepens our capacity for compassion.

Holding Space

Any discussion on compassion, kindness, and the interconnectedness of people is incomplete without addressing the concept of 'Holding Space'. This term, popularised by Heather Plett, author of *The Art of Holding Space*, involves walking alongside another person in their journey without judgment, making them feel inadequate, attempting to fix them, or controlling the outcome. Holding space entails opening our hearts, offering unconditional support, and relinquishing judgment and control.

Heather illustrates this concept by sharing her experience when her mother was terminally ill, and their palliative caregiver, Ann, played the role of holding space for Heather and her siblings while they, in turn, held space for their dying mother.

Heather emphasises the impossibility of being a strong space holder without others who can reciprocate. Even the most robust leaders, coaches, or nurses need a safe space where they can be vulnerable without fear of judgment.

Here are some key points Heather has learnt about holding space:

- Give people permission to trust their intuition and wisdom

- Provide information only in manageable amounts
- Empower others; don't take away their power
- Keep your ego out of it
- Create a safe space for failure
- Offer guidance with humility
- Foster a container for complex emotions, fear, or trauma
- Allow different decisions and experiences

Heather concludes that holding space is a complex practice that evolves with experience and is unique to each person and situation. It is not limited to coaches or facilitators; everyone can practice it for partners, children, friends, or even strangers.

Amid unprecedented challenges such as divisiveness, racism, and the lingering effects of the COVID-19 pandemic, Heather asserts that a revolution of compassion is needed. Holding space without judgment is crucial for navigating these turbulent times. She envisions a new global ethos emerging, grounded in shared humanity, interconnection, and compassion. In this envisioned future, our collective strength lies not in technology or artificial intelligence but in our shared sensitivity, kindness, and mutual dependence.

As musician Dame Evelyn Glennie eloquently puts it, 'We are all like little musical notes dotted around the planet, moving here and there just as a musician plays the dots they see on a score. Each note is a pearl when taken care of, just as we are all pearls in the stories we create and project. The linking of my musical note to your musical note is done through listening. My story with your story brings forth another story, and so it goes on and on.'

Practices

- Make it a practice to smile at strangers or people you meet on the streets. Don't worry about what they may think; just smile genuinely.

- Be curious about people you encounter daily, such as the security guard who takes care of your building or the boy who serves you tea.

- You may ask them about their lives and families.

- Every day, try to do some act of kindness. It can be a small act like an encouraging word or a pat on the back.

- Notice how you feel inside your body after an act of compassion.

- Do you feel good, warm, happy? Would you like to repeat it?

- Notice how you feel about it.

- When people ask you for help, how do you feel about it, what do you feel inside? Notice your reactions, and you can be sure that others feel the same way.

- Offer yourself kindness and compassion even if you have not met your own standards. Tell yourself that you tried your best and do not be too harsh.

- Are you a perfectionist and blame yourself for not getting things right? You need self-compassion the most. Allow yourself not to be perfect from time to time and let there be room for imperfection.

- Practise holding space for a friend, your partner, or kids. When they are upset or angry, be willing to just listen to them and let them vent out their feelings. No need to offer advice.

- Notice the way you speak to yourself. Is it too self-critical?
- Give yourself a healthy dose of self-compassion from time to time.
- Make a note of what you perceive to be your imperfections—anger, envy, or greed. Offer yourself compassion for these parts rather than rejecting them or denying them.
- Make a mental note of what you think to be the barriers to showing more kindness—it may be about what people may think, about society, or a feeling of awkwardness.
- See whether it is possible to bring about a more compassionate atmosphere in your workplace. Also notice the effect of kindness on the employees.
- Once in a while, on a leisurely day, you can set out with some spare money and donate it to someone on the roadside. Maybe give Rs 100 to someone you feel needs it. Don't bother about what the person may do with it; just give it.

12

SPACE AND SILENCE

'Space and silence are two aspects of the same thing, the same nothing. They are an externalization of inner space and inner silence, which is stillness: the infinitely creative womb of all existence.'
—Eckhart Tolle

$\mathcal{S}$itting in the audience, I was watching the slides and lectures on third space endoscopy, mesmerised. As a senior gastroenterologist, I had been practising endoscopy for the last fifteen years, but I couldn't help marvel at the recent progress being made in the area of third space endoscopy; a submucosal space had been created by what appeared to be magic out of thin air. The experts were explaining how, with the help of this third space, a tunnel could be created, and life-saving procedures could be performed which otherwise would have needed surgery.

I was invited by Dr Vikas Singla, one of the leading third space endoscopists in the country, to give a talk on well-being for doctors. While waiting for my turn and thinking about what to share with the audience, it struck me that when we become mindful and bring pauses into our hectic

191

lives, we also create such spaces within ourselves. This sense of spaciousness and stillness within us, even in the midst of hectic activity, can make a world of difference to our state of mind, happiness, and well-being. Just like the third space in endoscopy, this has always been within us. It is not artificially created, but only now have we learnt to make an opening into it.

The sense of spaciousness has fascinated me right from the time I started my mindfulness and meditation practice. Initially, I was asked by a friend how these measures were helping me, but I struggled to find the right words and simply said all I knew was that there was a growing sense of space within me which was absent before. It appeared to me that while everything externally was more or less the same, now there was more space to manoeuvre and respond to situations rather than react.

Space Is Not an Object

In his books, *A New Earth* and *The Power of Now*, Eckhart Tolle talks eloquently about this inner space. Tolle says that when we are no longer totally identified with form-consciousness, who we are becomes freed from its imprisonment in form. This freedom is the arising of inner space. It comes as a stillness, a subtle peace deep within us, even in the face of something seemingly unpleasant. Suddenly, there is space around the event. There is also space around the emotional highs and lows, even around pain. Above all, there is space between our thoughts.

From that space emanates an aliveness and tranquillity that feels peaceful and still. In fact, Eckhart, as well as many other masters, can bring alive this space within us by their words or mere presence. It has been my experience that whenever I read *The Power of Now*, I could feel within me the arising of space and stillness. This has been verified by numerous other readers as well. The great enlightened Indian saint, Ramana Maharshi, used to simply sit in silence while those around him would notice a deep shift arising within them. This is the power of presence.

It is not difficult to fathom why this happens if one delves deep. Physicists are now convinced that the solidity of matter is an illusion. Even seemingly solid matter, including our physical body, is nearly 99 per cent empty space—so vast are the distances between the atoms compared to their size. What is more, even inside every atom, there is mostly empty space. What is left is more like a vibrational frequency than particles of solid matter, much like a musical note, explains Eckhart Tolle. He explains that the unmanifested is present in this world as silence and space. Space can be easily missed, just like silence, since everybody pays attention to the things in space but not to space by itself. But the moment we make space into an object, we miss the whole point. Space is closest to our inner true nature of awareness, and just like awareness, we can become conscious of it but not by trying to convert it into a graspable object.

Cultivate More Space to Your Life

To nurture space consciousness and bring more space into our everyday lives, Eckhart suggests beginning by withdrawing attention from the objects in space and becoming aware of space itself. He uses the example of a room containing furniture, pictures, objects, and fans, where the essence of the room is the empty space. Similarly, we need to be aware of the space around us. Instead of thinking about it with the mind or trying to label it, simply pay attention to it and feel it. As awareness of this empty space deepens, a shift in consciousness takes place.

According to Eckhart, this shift occurs because the inner equivalent to objects in outer space, such as furniture and walls, are our mind objects—thoughts, emotions, and sense objects. The inner equivalent of space is consciousness or awareness that enables mind objects to be, just as outer space allows all things to be. By withdrawing attention from external things, we automatically withdraw attention from mind objects. This contemplation of space becomes a portal for the unmanifested.

Understanding these concepts doesn't require mental strain. When reading about them, they instantly appealed to me, and I could see how space plays a vital role in various aspects of our lives. As a passionate cricket fan and player, I reflected on how creating space while batting allowed for more powerful strikes. In the context of my medical practice, I recognised the importance of having breathing space when facing a busy schedule. Arriving early provides the extra time needed to complete work in a relaxed manner, preventing frustration and burnout.

In her book, *Finding the Space to Lead*, author and leadership coach Janice Marturano notes that leading CEOs desire more space even more than power or money. According to her survey, most people lack the breathing room necessary for clarity, focus, and deep listening to oneself and others. Living on a non-stop treadmill takes a toll, leading to a lack of creativity and connection. We need space to step off the treadmill, focus on what's essential, celebrate small joys, and be compassionate, tender, and fulfilled human beings.

Pause to Create More Space

Janice teaches her clients how to create these moments of space by cultivating purposeful pauses throughout the day. She defines this as a moment when you notice the swirl of the day and choose to intentionally pay attention. In the midst of a busy meeting, one may observe the rapid pace of racing thoughts, feeling mentally transported to another place. It becomes opportune to pause deliberately, heightening awareness of our breath and grounding ourselves by sensing the contact of our feet against the ground.

One moment of consciously becoming aware of our breath may be enough to snap out of the spell of autopilot thinking. We could interject a purposeful pause when our children are talking to us enthusiastically, while our attention is on striking off things from our to-do list. By recognising and intervening in these moments, we can redirect our focus and provide our children with our undivided attention in that particular moment.

In chapter 3, under the 'mindfulness on the go' section, I have listed many such examples of bringing about pauses in our daily lives to become present again. For me, this practice of pausing from time to time has been life-changing, which I will describe further in the next chapter. You may find your own versions of purposeful pauses and be able to create spaces and mindful moments in your schedule. These pauses are available to us at any moment on demand.

The Open Focus Method

The importance of space in our daily lives has been scientifically validated by Les Fehmi, director of Princeton Biofeedback Center and author of the *Open Focus Brain*. Through a random series of questions he discovered that when volunteers were asked, 'Can you imagine the space between your eyes?' or 'Can you imagine the space between your ears?' they achieved a notable augmentation in alpha brain synchrony at the monitored brain sites.

Fehmi asserts that the practice of objectless imagery, involving the multisensory experience and awareness of space, nothingness, or absence, consistently triggers extended and robust periods of phase-synchronous alpha activity. When brain waves peak and trough perfectly in time, they are said to be phase synchronous. Fehmi discovered that research had shown that phase-synchronous alpha waves were the hallmark of veteran meditators. He developed the

'Open Focus Attention' programme with sustained awareness of space as the guide point. In his guided exercises, he leads participants through different kinds of objectless imagery, asking them to imagine space around and through body regions, such as their eyes, neck, head, and hands.

Fehmi postulated that when the brain is processing sense objects, it uses high frequency, desynchronised beta activity. However, when the mind is asked to imagine or attend to space, there is nothing for the mind to objectify; thus, the cortical rhythm slips into slower alpha and later theta rhythms. He explains that awareness of space is a powerful tool to teach people to get into a relaxed yet alert state of functioning. Not only are we aware of the things around us, but there is also an awareness of space, silence, and a sense of timelessness.

He further expanded the use of this open focus space awareness in the management of pain. In the process of dissolving pain, patients are trained to initially focus on the painful stimuli and then bring their attention to the space in and around the pain point, moving and merging with the painful stimuli. In this process, Fehmi explains that pain is no longer held exclusively as an object at a distance in narrow focus, but rather our awareness has expanded to include the space around it.

In this manner, a space is created all around the painful stimuli. This is similar to what we had discussed earlier, in the chapter on emotions, about how when we become aware of our emotional symptoms—fear or sadness—we allow the emotions to be embraced by a space around it.

Narrow Focus vs Wide Focus

The importance of Les Fehmi's research is that it highlights the difference between narrow focus attention and wide focus attention. We have been trained to function with a narrow focus attention because it is more efficient in getting things done, but this is certainly at the cost of our wide focus attention, which takes in the whole picture and offers a spaciousness to the perception.

This difference is similar to our discussion about the Doing mode (narrow focus) vs the Being mode (wide focus). In his book *Open Focus Brain*, Fehmi suggests that we can learn to use the technique of open focus and apply it in our daily lives. Fehmi says, 'Whenever you think of it, carry out your everyday tasks while at the same time being aware of infinite space, silence, and timelessness. Be aware of the three-dimensional space between, around and through objects.' According to him, we should attend to all our senses—seeing, hearing, feeling, tasting, and smelling—and be aware of the background space that permeates everything. This helps to activate the right brain, open our attention, and loosen the grip of the left brain on our experience of the world, giving rise to a more open and relaxed feeling.

The Open Space of Awareness

In the chapter on mindfulness and creativity, we touched upon the open awareness method of meditation, which can now be better understood through the concept of open focus attention. In this method, we do not focus on any particular object of attention; instead, we allow everything to unfold in a space of open awareness.

The spiritual master Adyashanti also describes this method as true meditation. According to him, 'true meditation' is allowing our awareness to be as it is without trying to manipulate or control it. All objects—thoughts, feelings, emotions, and sensations—are left to their natural functioning. Rather than being aware of our breath or an object, the idea is to rest in a space of open awareness. Abiding in this state of open receptivity, free of any goal or anticipation, facilitates the presence of stillness and spaciousness, which stands revealed as our natural condition.

Non-Judgemental Space

This open spaciousness doesn't judge or label; it is all-inclusive and accepting. There is space for our negative thoughts and emotions, our so-called bad habits or vices, as well as, of course, for all that is good and wholesome in us. I remember attending a five-day silent retreat held by Adyashanti near London in 2016. It was a defining moment for me because I had to take almost two weeks off from work in India to attend the silent retreat in the United Kingdom. I had to convince my family, and I could clearly see the surprised looks on the faces of my friends and colleagues when I informed them about my decision. I was convinced that, to live my life more wholeheartedly, I needed to make this trip. It was a wonderful experience, and I loved every minute of it.

When the retreat was over, we celebrated by dancing and with a spread of delicious food, including meats and drinks at a friend's house. I was enjoying myself fully and indulged in all the fun and food. I remember one of my friend's wives asking me in astonishment, 'Saroj, I can't understand you; you have come all the way to London for a spiritual retreat, and after the retreat, you are enjoying all these non-spiritual things. Isn't it paradoxical and totally contradictory?'

I'm not sure exactly what I told her, but I didn't find anything contradictory in it. I believe that there is space for everything. Savouring life's pleasures healthily and moderately will do us no harm. We don't have to set rigid guidelines about spirituality and doing anything other than that is crossing the line. All of this can unfold without judgment or the need to turn it into a significant issue requiring fixing.

Spaciousness in Nature

I also began to comprehend the reason behind my deep love for the beach and water bodies when I read more about spaciousness. As a family, we love going to the beaches for holidays. After a rejuvenating dip in the sea, there's nothing

I cherish more than reclining on a sunbed, marvelling at the breathtaking expanse of the sea and crystal-clear blue water. The extensive stretch of glistening sand on the beach, harmoniously contrasted with the boundless expanse of the radiant blue sky above, adds to the spectacle. This was nothing short of heaven, and I could sit like that for hours. While holidaying in the hills, I would get the same pleasure and joy on beholding the mountains, the sky, and the land beneath. I'm sure many of you have experienced this same joy and pleasure. One reason why we enjoy this sight is that it resonates with our true nature of vastness that shines on such occasions of relaxed enjoyment.

Having glimpsed this spaciousness, there's no need to constantly seek refuge in mountains or beaches; rather, we should simply cultivate an awareness of space in our everyday lives—whether it's the room around us, the space between people, or the gaps between our thoughts. The more we attune ourselves to the space external to us, the more expansive we become within.

Niksen—The Art of Doing Nothing

In our extremely hectic lives, what we need more than anything is space and time to do nothing. There is a wonderful term in Dutch named 'Niksen', which can be described as the 'Art of Doing Nothing.' Olga Mecking, author of *Niksen: Embracing the Dutch Art of Doing Nothing*, elaborates on this in her book. The idea of niksen is to take conscious, considered time and energy to do activities like gazing out of the window or sitting motionless and simply giving ourselves space. As a society, we pride ourselves on our ability to keep doing things and being busy all the time, and hence stopping the cycle of busyness can be a challenging concept.

Psychologist Doreen Dodgen-Magee likens niksen to a car whose engine is running but isn't going anywhere. Olga Mecking provides useful guidance on practising niksen in our lives. Her suggestion is that if you are doing nothing, own it, and if someone asks you what you're doing during a nothing break, simply respond, 'Nothing.' Be unapologetic about taking breaks or holidays, and if you start feeling guilty about being seen as lazy, think of niksen not as a sign of laziness but as an important life skill.

Choose the initial discomfort of niksen over the familiarity of busyness. It is important to note that niksen is not just about sitting still, which may not be everyone's cup of tea. You may go for a stroll or just sit idle without any particular aim or goal. Olga advises us to take out moments of niksen throughout the day, whether at work, home, or commuting. The more we practise these moments, the greater the chances of it developing into an ingrained habit.

She also recommends having a 'niksen space' at home in the form of an armchair or sofa or simply a space on the couch, making it easy for engaging in it. Canadian journalist Rachel Jonat in *The Joy of Doing Nothing* gives a unique suggestion of preparing a 'not-to-do list' in contrast to the ubiquitous 'to-do list'. The whole idea is to find things you want to stop doing and free up the time. When I read about niksen, it struck a chord immediately, especially about the niksen space. In my house, there is a corner where I have kept a mattress and pillow, and for me, that is my sacred niksening place. Everyone is very familiar with that corner, and when someone vists me, they know where to find me in my spare time. Given the chance, I can spend hours in that place doing nothing or niksening, and these are some of my most joyful moments.

We need to consciously choose to take out some time for niksen, no matter how chaotic our schedules are. Jenny Odell, author of *How to do Nothing*, coined the acronym NOMO, 'Necessity for missing out', which is similar to another acronym I love, JOMO or 'Joy of missing out'. When we choose to make out some time for niksen rather than packing our days with endless activities, we can feel a sense of joy and lightness. Olga also emphasises that while it may sound like mindfulness, niksen is not the same. While mindfulness has a certain format to it like being aware of one's breathing and being present, niksen is just doing nothing. There is no need to split hairs about these terms, but simply cherish these moments of non-doing and spaciousness and cultivate more of it in our daily life.

Sky-Gazing Meditation and Space

In Tibetan Buddhism, there is a meditation practice called sky-gazing, derived from the Dzogchen tradition, emphasising resting in a natural state free from conceptual elaborations. This state is wide open, clear, and lucid—neither rejecting nor clinging to anything—and is sometimes referred to as spontaneous awareness. It is spontaneous because it has always existed, called primordial awareness.

Chad Foreman, a meditation and mindfulness teacher, explains that the clear blue sky closely resembles this natural state. Like the sky unaffected by passing weather, our natural state remains unstained by thoughts or emotions, regardless of their intensity.

Pure from the beginning, this natural state aims to connect individuals to the vast, expansive, clear, open space of awareness—their authentic nature. Engaging in sky-gazing brings relaxation, peace, joy, and a fresh sense of connecting to reality, the natural state of things. Present awareness is empty, open, luminous, and lucid.

Chad notes that while this meditation is intended for high-up places, it can be done anywhere, even at your computer. The space in front of you and between you and the computer can serve as a shift of attention from objects to clear open space.

Addictions, Seeking, and the Space of Presence

In his book, *Natural Rest for Addiction*, Scott Kiloby discusses resting and relaxing in the open space of presence, termed natural rest, as a profound way of healing from any addiction. Scott, who fought various addictions throughout his adult life, found a permanent solution in repeatedly resting in presence. This involves allowing thoughts, emotions, cravings, and energies to be as they are, leading to the eventual release of the addictive cycle.

Addictions are not limited to substances but can extend to work, relationships, eating, shopping, vacations, or even constant thinking. Many are unaware of the addiction to constant mental activity. Scott emphasises that seeking to avoid unpleasant feelings and thoughts by constantly looking to the future perpetuates the cycle of seeking relief from restlessness and feelings of lack or boredom.

Scott contends that addiction is an unfillable hole in our lives. Moments of release or satisfaction from quenching urges are temporary, and the seeking cycle prevails. The solution, according to Scott, lies in the present moment's space called natural rest, into which we need to relax.

Repeatedly resting in this space naturally stops the seeking of the future. This restful presence permeates every aspect of our lives, providing rest, freedom, and well-being where the cycle of addictive seeking has trapped us.

As addicts—in various forms—what we seek more than anything else is the end of seeking itself, according to Scott. Relaxing into the space of the present moment allows us to find the resolution of our seeking, right here, right now—the one place often overlooked.

The sense of spaciousness within us increases when we are present, centred, and grounded. Being centred and present leads to feeling more spacious, creating a chain reaction. In a simple experiment, when you are present and relaxed, entering a room allows you to take in the entire ambience, including objects and the space, while entering hurriedly or stressed narrows your focus to the immediate task or person, neglecting the room's other contents or space.

The Sound of Silence

Space and silence are two aspects of the same thing—the same nothing, as explained by Eckhart in *The Power of Now*. They are an externalisation of inner space and silence, which is stillness—the infinite creative womb of all existence. Eckhart mentions that, like space, silence can be a portal to the unmanifest. He advises that from time to time, we need to pay more attention to silence than to sounds. Paying attention to outer silence creates inner silence; the mind becomes still, and a portal opens up.

In the same book, he points out that every sound is born out of silence, dies back into silence, and during its lifespan is surrounded by silence. It is an intrinsic but unmanifested part of every sound, every musical note, every song. This simple but beautiful quote profoundly sums it up: 'Nothing in this world is so like God as silence.' Even during a conversation, we should become conscious of the gaps between words, the brief interval between silence. Doing so makes the dimension of stillness grow within us. Throughout the ages, saints and teachers have waxed eloquent about silence. Adyashanti says: 'Silence is the only teaching and the only teacher that is there all the time.'

My relationship with silence has evolved gradually over the years. By nature, I have been fun-loving, extroverted, and enjoyed socialising. Not to sound immodest, but I was often hailed as the life of the party, taking the onus of breaking awkward pauses and silences during conversations by injecting humour or liveliness. After coming across Eckhart's work, I started appreciating the role of silence, and once I began meditating, I truly understood how powerful it was. Since then, I have attended numerous retreats of Mooji and

Adyashanti, most of them being silent sittings, giving access to an expansive state always present within us. Now when people ask me for advice on mindfulness or meditation, I often suggest spending a few minutes a day just sitting in silence. It can be as short as two minutes, simply enjoying the silence and letting whatever has to happen take place. Once you can sit in silence alone, you can bring that inner silence into the marketplace. It can be the noisiest and most chaotic place, yet you can experience a stillness and silence within, which is beautiful and profound. One of the most amazing and liberating experiences for me is to be in a place of chaos, frenzy, and noise like the airport or hospital and yet be still and silent within.

Types of Silence

I love the way Norton Juster, author of *The Phantom Tollbooth*, describes the various kinds of silence in his book. 'Have you ever heard the wonderful silence just before the dawn? Or the quiet and calm just as a storm ends? Perhaps you know the silence when you haven't the answer to a question you've been asked, the hush of a country road at night, or the expectant pause of a room full of people when someone is just about to speak, or most beautiful of all, the moment after the door closes and you're alone in the whole house? Each one is different, you know, and all very beautiful if you listen carefully.'

We normally assume that silence is just the absence of sound, but when we become still and present, we realise that similar to the variety of sounds we hear, there are myriad hues of silence, which can be quite profound. Novelist, poet, and psychotherapist Paul Goodman also identified nine kinds of silence in his classic book, *Speaking and Language: Defence of Poetry*, ranging from the noisy silence of resentment, the baffled silence of confusion to the musical silence that accompanies absorbed activity and the profound fertile silence of awareness.

The Gift of Silent Presence

Silence can be extremely comforting and therapeutic at times when words may seem superfluous, even damaging. Celebrated author Parker Palmes talks about this in the article, 'The Gift of Presence, the Perils of Advice'. During his bout with deep depression, he discusses how well-meaning friends would come up with several suggestions and solutions, which only made him feel more isolated. He explains that the human soul doesn't want to be advised or fixed or saved. It simply wants to be witnessed—to be seen, heard, and companioned exactly as it is. However, companioning takes time and patience, which we often lack, especially in the presence of painful suffering that we seem unable to stand.

He describes that during this painful phase one of his friends, Bill, saved his life with the comfort of his silent presence. He describes how Bill would come to his house daily at 4 p.m. and massage his feet. He rarely said a word, but Parker could somehow feel a sense of connection only in this silent presence.

All of us have experienced this treasure of silent presence. I remember being in a state of shock and distress for a few days after my father's death. Even getting up seemed to be a great effort. I would simply lie on the bed, and I distinctly remember a distant relative of mine who came and sat there in silence for nearly the whole day. He also attended to basic tasks like making arrangements to shift the body, while I was allowed to grieve in silence. I found his silent presence soothing and remember it vividly to this day.

Music and Silence

Most artists and musicians have understood the magic and power of silence and use it to highlight their music. The celebrated genius Mozart expressed it beautifully by saying, 'The music is not in the notes but in the silence between'. The celebrated 20th-century pianist Arthur Rubinstein was once asked to reveal the secret behind his outstanding music. He simply said, 'I handle notes no better than many pianists. But the pauses between the notes ah, that is where the art resides.'

The great musicians tap into this field of silence knowing that it is the womb from which the next note is created. Indian classical music is famous for using eloquent pauses that transport the listener into a meditative sublime state. The famous Indian mystical master Osho conveys this brilliantly in a talk on silence and music: 'Between sounds of music, there are gaps of silence. The authentic music consists not of sounds, but of the gaps. Sounds come and go; those gaps remain. And music can make you aware of those gaps more beautifully than anything else; hence I have to say that music comes next to silence.'

As a society, we have developed such a fascination for objects, sounds, doing things, and keeping ourselves busy that we hardly give any importance to space, beingness, and silence in our lives. Probably, this is the reason behind our anxiety and restlessness despite being accustomed to all kinds of luxury and material comforts. This should tell us that we need to maintain a balance and bring more stillness into our lives. Space and silence are important portals into the unmanifest, the formless dimension which is our essential true nature. It pervades all aspects of our experience, and all we need to do is to pay attention to the background screen of space and silence, which allows all experience to take place. Adyashanti brilliantly describes it this way: 'There's a great space in which this moment takes place. There's a great silence that is listening to the thoughts.'

Practices

- Can you imagine the space between your eyes? Reflect on this for a minute and visualise it.

- Can you imagine the space between your ears? Reflect on this question and imagine the space.

- See if you can imagine the space between your fingers and toes.

- Look at the page you are reading, be aware of not just the printed words but the background space. Be aware of the space between you and the computer screen.

- Look at the sky and the space all around you, look at clouds or stars and the space between them.

- Focus on an object on a table, then focus on the space of the room where the table is kept.

- For the sky-gazing meditation, you can sit in your balcony, in your room, or if possible, outside in the open sky and simply be aware of the sky and let your awareness merge with the space of the sky.

- When you have the urge to drink or smoke, just stay with the feeling. Observe if that craving gradually dissipates.

- Observe the feeling of a sense of lack or incompleteness. Notice how, if left to itself, the feeling will dissolve in the space of aware presence. Simply stay with that feeling of lack or emptiness for even 30 seconds and see how it feels. Then extend it a little more.

- Get used to moments of silence. Just sit in silence without any agenda. Start with two minutes. You may feel restless at first, but then you will get used to it, and an inner stillness will develop. Do it from time to time throughout the day.

- Be aware of the gap between thoughts, the silence between words. This creates space consciousness.

- See if you can sit in silence for a few minutes with your friend, or spouse without the need for words to complete the moment.

- Be aware of the background silence of things, like the background silence of music or any sound which you may hear.

- Notice any sound like the barking of a dog and how it emerges from silence and dies back into silence.

- Notice the stillness of a tree or flower. When we become aware of stillness in an object, we become still inside.

- Next time when there is a power cut and the AC or fan stops, just notice the stillness as the sound of the AC or fan subsides. Then, notice the sounds when the AC starts again.

- Try to sit with restlessness. How often have you tried staying with the discomfort of restlessness? Observe how it fades when you allow yourself to stay with it without trying to change it.

- Take out some time for niksen in your life, maybe an hour a day.

- Make a 'not-to-do' list. Include things you would prefer not to waste time doing so that you can do more of what you like.

13

THE MAGIC OF HABITS

*'Consistency is an underappreciated form of
unintentional magic disguised as a mundane doing.'*
—**Victoria Erickson**

I could hear the sound of excited voices, animated discussions, and hysterical laughter as, one after the other, my friends trickled into the common room. Around 15 of us from our medical college, CMC Vellore, had gathered for a mini-reunion—a boys-only party—in Goa. We had booked an exotic villa and were looking forward to a weekend of unadulterated fun, hoping to recreate the magic and madness of our hostel days.

Sanjay entered my room with a beer bottle in one hand and shouted excitedly, 'Hey, Saroj, aren't you ready yet? Let's go for breakfast. What the hell . . .' he stopped midway in disbelief. He had found me sitting on the bed, eyes closed, meditating. I looked up, smiled sheepishly, and explained, 'Just give me a few minutes; I will finish and come over soon. It's a habit, actually . . .' I added lamely, trying to pacify him.

Sanjay shook his head in disbelief and went out. I could hear him yelling to someone, 'Listen, Saroj has gone totally nuts, I tell you.' I smiled to myself and soon went to join the others. By the end of the day, I had atoned for my lunacy—by their standards—by having a real blast of a time.

Meditation had become a lifelong habit with me, and whether working or holidaying, a consistent habit never leaves your side. I was drawn to write this chapter on habits not only because the cultivation of various habits has been rewarding for me, but it is an integral part of the growth and success of any great person we can think of.

'If you can get just one per cent better each day for one year, you end up 37 times better by the time the year is over. This is the magic of compounding,' declares James Clear, author of *The Atomic Habits*. He summarises it brilliantly by saying: 'Habits are the compound interest of self-improvement.'

In his book, he gives numerous examples to support this. He starts with the example of the British cycling coach Brailsford, who had been hired in 2003 to put the British cycling team on a new trajectory. His strategy was novel and simple but profoundly rewarding. He referred to his formula as the 'aggregation of marginal gains,' which was the philosophy of searching for a tiny margin of improvement in everything you do. His idea was that if you broke down everything that you could think of in riding a bike and then improved it by one per cent, there would be significant improvements when you put them together. This was the reason behind the stupendous subsequent success of the British cycling team in all formats.

Any financial person can tell you about the magic of compounding in money, but not too many people understand the life-transforming effects small daily changes can make in our lives. This is also true for bad habits, and our faulty eating habits, lack of exercise, and procrastination can slowly accumulate and have harmful effects over time. According to the business magnate and famous investor Warren Buffet, 'Chains of habit are too light to be felt until they are too heavy to be broken.'

The seed of every habit is a single, tiny decision. A habit may be defined as a behaviour that has been repeated enough times to become automatic. James Clear explains the reason behind the term 'atomic habits', suggesting that habits are like the atoms of our lives, each one being a fundamental unit that contributes to our improvement. Atomic habits imply a regular practice or routine that is not only small and manageable but is also the source of incredible power over time.

The concept of small habits having powerful results when performed consistently resonated deeply with me. Despite possessing only average intelligence, I have consistently excelled in numerous competitive exams since childhood. The key to my success, which I am eager to share, lies in the cultivation of disciplined and steadfast habits. When I was preparing for my medical entrance exams, it was about consistently making studying every day a habit and meticulously planning the way to approach each exam.

I have waged a seesaw battle with my weight since childhood and often successfully lost up to 15–20 kgs through the same formula of consistently following a regimen of diet, exercise, or both. Once you start getting results, it can motivate you in other unrelated areas, too.

I remember, around 15 years ago when I initially started meditating, I wanted to incorporate it into my busy life because I could see how favourably it was impacting me in every aspect. Recalling my earlier success in competitive exams and weight loss, I thought I could apply some of those principles here as well. I decided to start by dedicating a small, manageable time to the practice—five or ten minutes every day.

Within six months, I was able to extend that time to half an hour by decreasing my sleeping time a bit, and now I spend two to three hours a day meditating despite my hectic work schedule. I have always believed that the ability to do something consistently over a long period is the most rewarding skill. Take the example of any world-class sportsman like Sachin Tendulkar or Virat Kohli, and you will find that behind their spectacular success has been a consistent dedication to practising and honing their skills.

Habit Loop

In the book *Atomic Habits*, James Clear lists four steps to building powerful habits.

1. Cue: It triggers your brain to initiate a behaviour. It is a bit of information that predicts a reward. The cue is the first indication that we are close to a reward, it naturally leads to craving. For example, the cue may be to step out for a jog or gym after you have had your morning tea.

2. Cravings: They are the motivational force behind every habit. The smoker craves smoking because he craves the feeling of relief it provides. The thoughts, feelings, and emotions of the observer are what transforms a cue into a craving.

3. Response: It is the actual habit you perform that can take the form of a thought or an action.

4. Reward: Finally, the response delivers a reward. Rewards are the end goal of every habit. The cue is about noticing the reward, the craving is about wanting the reward, and the response is about obtaining the reward.

Together, these four steps allow us to create automatic habits and this cycle is known as the 'habit loop'. In his book, Clear creates a framework based on the four steps that he refers to as the 'four laws of behaviour changes' that help you to create new habits and break bad ones.

The book is a must-read for anyone interested in building new habits or eliminating destructive ones from their lives. Irrespective of age, status, or schedule, anyone can apply these steps and reap the benefits which are applicable in all fields of life. Whenever you want to create a new habit, you should simply ask yourself these questions:

- How can I make it obvious?
- How can I make it attractive?
- How can I make it easy?
- How can I make it satisfying?

The Habit of Marginal Improvements

It's about one step. An enriching habit I've cultivated over the years is listening to inspiring TED Talks and motivational videos. One such unforgettable talk was Stephen Duneier's TED talk. Duneier describes his journey from being a seventh-grade student with a C- average grade, struggling to focus for more than five to ten minutes at a time, to his extraordinary transformation into the Head of Currency Option Trading at Bank of America and subsequently a Guinness record holder. He attributes his successful trajectory to his personalised approach and habits to achieve his goals.

Duneier's approach focuses on breaking down large goals into a step-by-step series of small decisions. The secret to Duneier's success, in his own words: 'All I do is take really big, ambitious projects that people seem to marvel at, break them down to their simplest form, and then just make marginal improvements along the way to improve my odds of achieving them.'

His breakthrough came in high school when, faced with an inability to focus for even a few minutes resulting in a string of poor scores, he made a novel decision to adjust marginally. If he had to complete five chapters, he would break it down to the smallest manageable task, not even one chapter but just three or four paragraphs, whatever he could focus on at a time.

From that point forward all the way through to graduation, Duneier was a straight-A student, President's Honor Roll in every semester, and then went on to graduate in a top programme in finance and economics. Subsequently, he replicated this same formula in his career. The central theme—take big concepts, complex ideas, huge assignments, and break them down into much more manageable tasks.

Reaping extraordinary success in his career, Duneier began to apply this formula to other aspects of his life. He observed that each day he would spend walking up and down for 45 minutes each way, so he decided to utilise this time—which he just spent listening to music—into learning German at a relatively old age. He followed this up by earning his auto racing license, learning how to fly a helicopter, rock-climbing, skydiving, and flying planes aerobatically. He achieved all of this by making a minor adjustment to his routine.

In his talk, he explains that if you are planning to go on a marathon for 30 miles, it's not about 30 miles, nor even about one mile but about one step. Even before that step, it's about deciding when you are plonked in front of the TV set or computer to get up and tie your shoelaces. He summarises it succinctly: 'You pick up a book and you read one word. If you read one word, you'll read two words, three words; you'll read a sentence, a paragraph, a page, a chapter, a book; you'll read 10 books, 30 books, 50 books.'

These are simple yet incredibly powerful tools to enhance the quality of our lives. James Clear's message of one per cent improvement on a consistent basis and Stephen Duneier's amazing success story motivated me to make many small changes in my life. I had recently shifted to a high-rise building, and our apartment was on the eighth floor. I decided that I would climb three or four flights of stairs daily whenever I had to enter or leave my house, while for the rest I would use the elevator. If I could do this every day, it would definitely have health benefits over a period of time.

I had tremendously enjoyed listening to inspiring talks and videos in my spare time, but I was now motivated to make it a daily habit while jogging, going for walks, or sitting behind in the car. Even if I listened just 10 minutes at a time, it amounted to around 45 minutes of inspiring stuff, and that over a period of a year would enrich my life a lot. I applied the same formula to reading as well, even if it were one page or two pages at a time. My Kindle library boasts well over 900 books now, and much of the material of this book, which you are reading, has been gathered from the information from these talks and books.

I was earlier under the misconception that it was not possible to read consistently after a certain age, as work and family take up all the time, but now I have learnt that one can find the time to do anything with slight adjustments in our lifestyle. We just need to set an intention, start with something small and manageable, but do it on a consistent basis.

Don't Break the Chain

When talking to a rookie comedian who wanted to make a name, the famous comedian Jerry Seinfeld told him that in order to be successful, he should spend some time every single day developing new material, even if he wasn't feeling up to it. The important thing was to never miss a day—to never break the chain—to continue improving.

This motivational technique aids daily commitment to any desired habit. Initiating a new habit often involves an initial burst of enthusiasm, which tends to wane after a week, as research confirms. This is where Seinfeld's advice becomes pertinent. When he was trying to make it in the world of comedy, Seinfeld displayed a large calendar in his apartment and vowed to write at least one joke every day. After he completed this task, he would mark the day with a red X, creating a visual chain of consistency. We can draw inspiration from these effective tips and apply them to our lives.

Tremendous Tiny Habits

Similar to the methods discussed earlier is the concept of 'tiny habits' developed by B. J. Fogg. Fogg is the founder of Behavior Design Lab at Stanford University, and he developed the tiny habits method based on his research and coaching. His research revealed there were mainly three ways people could create lasting changes—have an epiphany, change the environment, or make tiny changes to their habits.

In this method, Fogg focuses on small actions achievable in less than 30 seconds. This way, new habits can be wired in quickly, growing naturally. He advocates starting with one or two small behaviours. 'Tiny,' says Fogg, 'allows you to start right now and meets you right where you are.' Examples include uttering positive affirmations when placing feet on the floor each morning or committing to two push-ups after flushing the toilet. According to Fogg, he found that the only consistent, sustainable way to grow big is to start small. One tiny action might feel insignificant at first, but it allows you to gain the momentum needed to tackle more significant challenges and make faster progress. He also emphasises celebrating successes, however insignificant, as feeling successful helps wire in new habits and motivates further efforts. The three-step method of the Anatomy of Tiny Habits is:

1. Anchor moment: Couple your new habit to an existing routine like brushing your teeth or tying your shoelaces.

2. New tiny behaviour: Start with a simple version of the new habit you want like doing two push-ups.

3. Instant celebration: Mentally verbalise 'congrats' or 'good job', or give yourself a small treat.

You can use these methods to design new tiny habits to suit your requirement. In order to practise being more mindful and present in daily life, I devised the following tiny habits to incorporate in my schedule. In my classes on mindfulness, I guide others to try out tiny habits to make lasting changes. A few examples of these are:

a. Whenever I wash my hands, I become aware of the sensation of water on my hands.

b. When I open the door of a room or my car, I mentally say 'opening door', which brings me back to the present moment.

c. While answering the phone or reading a message, I say 'present' or 'reading.'

d. Whenever I sit on my chair, I say 'sitting down' and am aware that I am sitting and feel my back against the chair or sofa.

e. Every hour, I set a reminder to take three slow breaths, and be aware that I am breathing.

A common complaint among people is about paucity of time, so I always advise them to start small. Make a resolution to practice two or three minutes of mindful breathing to start with, perhaps two minutes twice a day. Once you have accomplished this tiny habit for a week, increase it every week by a minute or two, and soon after a couple of months you may be able to meditate for ten minutes a day without much of a struggle.

One of the most inspiring examples of developing a meditation habit is that of my driver, Mukherji. While he is an exceedingly efficient driver and a fine person, he used to suffer from severe anxiety and panic attacks. He overheard me discussing meditation with one of my friends and requested me to help him with some simple techniques. Without much hope to be honest, I taught him some simple steps.

A few days later, he informed me that he had commenced meditating for ten minutes, finding it both useful and relaxing. Almost two months later, I was amazed when he proudly declared that he now meditates for up to 45 minutes each day. He attributed this practice to significantly aiding him in his struggle with anxiety, self-defeating thoughts, and panic attacks. Over the course of several years, it remains a remarkable sight to observe my driver meditating while waiting in the car, a marked contrast to most drivers who spend their time in idle conversation or aimless gossip. I frequently reference his example to motivate others, emphasising that it is a straightforward practice, requiring only a resolute intention.

The Zorro Circle

In his book *The Happiness Advantage*, Shawn Achor talks about a concept called the 'Zorro circle' and the ways we can use it to achieve our most ambitious goals. According to him, one of the strongest drivers of our performance and success is the belief that our behaviour matters, that we have some control over the future. If we concentrate our efforts on small but manageable goals, we can regain the feeling of control so crucial to our performance.

Shawn advises that we first become aware of our strengths and weaknesses, and then identify which aspects of the situation we have control over and which we do not. Breaking down the task to smaller, more manageable goals helps us feel in control, builds our confidence, and keeps us committed.

This attitude helps in developing new habits and making it a part of our schedule. Whether it is running a marathon, writing a book, or joining a dance class, we need to bring it into our zone of control—the Zorro circle—and make incremental steps towards a greater goal.

The 20-Second Rule: The Path of Least Resistance

Another powerful method Shawn advocates to turn bad habits into good ones is to minimise barriers to change. Habits form because our brain changes in response to frequent practise, he reveals. An important point to note about habits is that as humans we are often drawn to the path of least resistance, to those things that are easy, convenient, and habitual. It is difficult to overcome this inertia.

The inertia, often referred to as activation energy, must be overcome to initiate a positive habit. Otherwise, human nature tends to lead us down the path of least resistance repeatedly, reverting to old habits like snacking, reaching for the TV remote, and slacking off. The twenty-second rule proposes that we reduce the barriers to change to just 20 seconds, which might be sufficient to establish a new life habit. Placing the desired behaviour on the path of least resistance is essential, making it require less energy and effort to initiate the habit.

If you plan to start running, keep your running shoes where you will immediately find them, rather than wasting time searching for them and losing enthusiasm. When I decided to wake up early and start my meditation practice, I would keep the required materials to make tea in an accessible place overnight so that I wouldn't lose time looking for them and lose the inclination to start the practice.

Shawn suggests that we need to lower the activation energy for habits we want to adopt and raise it for the habits we want to avoid. In his book *The Paradox of Choice* Barry Schwartz explains how setting rules in advance can free us from the constant barrage of willpower depleting choices that make a real difference in our lives. We may set rules in advance to limit our coffee intake to two cups a day or snacking to only once a day.

Kaizen

Making small changes on a consistent basis is the foundation of Kaizen, a Japanese philosophy. It is a means of making great and lasting change through small, steady increments. Its practical roots are based on the Japanese management concept for incremental—gradual, continuous—change—improvement, breaking tasks into small, manageable steps. It is also about finding new, creative, and effective ways to improve one's life, from tackling the mundane to managing stress to attaining our life vision.

Kaizen originated in lean manufacturing and the principles of the Toyota Way. The primary objective of Kaizen is to implement incremental changes within a company, addressing one issue at a time. The aim is to generate improvements that continuously update employees and systems in line with modern advancements.

Presently, it serves as a vital competitive strategy pillar in numerous successful companies globally.

Positive Emotions and Habits

Positive outlook and emotions are not necessarily innate; however, like any other habit, we can nurture these habits over time. Barbara Fredrickson, research scientist and author of the *Positivity* has dedicated a substantial part of her life to study positive emotions. We discussed her work in the chapter on awe and wonder earlier. Fredrickson offers proof that positivity opens us to the moment, broadening our outlook and making it more expansive.

In her book, she discusses the 'Open Heart' study and

how positivity helps in building enduring mental habits of openness. Greater positivity in the participants, she found, helped establish more open-minded mental habits after three months. The participants became habitually more aware of their surroundings, more mindful, and more open to possibilities. She concluded that, over time, positivity can create enduring mental habits.

Therefore, with a slight shift in our thinking, we can choose to develop positive mental habits like gratitude, compassion, mindfulness, and more. Over time, these habits multiply and become integral parts of our lives.

My Personal Habit Story

Even before delving into these remarkable books on habits, I always considered myself a creature of habits and was fascinated by their power. During my school years, I stumbled upon an article describing Benjamin Franklin's habit tracker. He had created a list of 13 virtues, such as temperance, silence, resolution, and sincerity, and each day he marked which virtues he was able to follow, tracking his progress.

Being a great admirer of Mahatma Gandhi, I have immersed myself in his books since childhood, particularly awestruck by the way he cultivated habits like truth, nonviolence, and silence. Over the past few years, I have developed significant powerful habits, which I would like to enumerate below, hoping it may inspire you to pursue new habits as well. Some of these have been mentioned earlier in the chapter, and I'll just touch upon them here.

1. Daily doses of inspiration: As mentioned earlier, I have made a conscious habit of imbibing some form of inspiration every day, either in the form of listening to TED talks, videos, or books. The more I read and listen, the more I come up with stimulating new ideas

and insights. At some point, there arose in me the desire to put down whatever I had learnt in writing, and that's how this book took shape. There was a lot of trepidation about the project, but I decided to use the secret of marginal improvement. I started by writing 100 or 200 words daily to kick-start the process, while on Sundays or holidays, I would write up to 1,000 or 1,500 words. As chapters started getting written, it provided the desired momentum and inspiration to write even more.

2. Early morning meditation: This has been one of the major blessings of my life, because initially it appeared impossible to start the day early and find time for meditation in my schedule. I have earlier described how I started meditating consistently for 10 minutes a day but after experiencing its benefits, I began devoting more time to it by cutting down on sleep. Now, I manage to wake up at five in the morning, do an hour or so of meditation, which is a great way to start my day. Ironically, even with less sleep time and more interruptions due to hospital phone calls, I feel more rested than before.

3. Pausing and being present: A life-changing practice for me has been to become more present and mindful. It took some time for this to develop into a habit and is still in the process of evolving. Apart from the scheduled mindfulness practice, I devised several ways to include mindfulness in my daily activities, such as being mindful while washing hands, opening doors, or while walking. I realised that the more I became mindful of small activities, the more it grew into a desirable habit. Another practice is to take deliberate pauses throughout the day. When I reach a destination like the hospital or clinic, I just sit for a couple of minutes in presence and awareness and anchor myself

to the moment. These small pauses allow me to stop the busyness of 'doing' for a moment and come to the 'being' mode.

4. Savouring: This has been discussed in the chapter on happiness, and I have found this to be an incredible yet simple practice. Whenever I see or experience anything that is pleasurable, I try to savour that feeling for a few more seconds, like watching a beautiful sunrise, exquisite architecture, or even enjoying a delicious snack. When we make a habit of savouring and taking in the good, life appears magical. We experience the rapture of simply being alive.

5. Waiting and breathing: We spend a huge part of our lives waiting—at traffic signals, elevators, or in queues. I find it extremely soothing to connect with my breath and being present during this waiting period, rather than being lost in thoughts or scrolling on the phone. This habit took some effort to develop since we are conditioned to be impatient and restless, and I am still learning the ropes. The breath always takes us away from the chatter and discursive noise of the mind and back to the present moment. One moment of consciously being aware of one's breath creates a gap amidst the incessant activity of the mind.

These are just a few examples of habits that I have successfully implemented in my life, with the hallmark being starting small and simple, but doing it consistently. They have enriched my life beyond measure, and I am sure you, too, can devise small yet extraordinary new habits.

―――✧◈✧―――

Consistency defines us. The habits we choose today integrate into our lives over the years. Thus, it's crucial to mindfully select our habits. Habits, akin to financial capital, are investments that yield returns in the future. Reflecting on whether one habit alone can transform our lives may seem unlikely, but what if we adopted another? And another?

James Clear asserts in *The Atomic Habits* that our lives can be transformed by seemingly innocuous choices—making small new habits. He emphasises that the holy grail of habit change lies in a multitude of tiny improvements, each constituting a fundamental unit of the overall system.

Initially, a tiny habit, such as reading one line of a book or meditating for two minutes, may appear insignificant. Yet, with consistent perseverance, life's scales start to tilt. We become aware of subtle changes within, motivating us to persist until we reach a tipping point.

Examining our lives, we can identify areas for minor adjustments. Considering the new habits we wish to cultivate and integrating them into our schedules is essential. The beauty lies in starting now, right where we are. Adding one extra stair climb or learning one new word a day takes no extra time. Over time, looking back reveals remarkable progress through the power of compounding, of tiny atomic habits.

Practices

- Embark on a new habit today using the tiny habit method; initiate with just two minutes daily. Maintain a journal to track your progress.

- As you place your foot on the ground each morning, affirm to yourself, 'Today will be a great day' or 'Today, I will learn something new.'

- Cultivate the practice of developing one tiny habit every week. By year-end, you will have established numerous new habits.

- Compile a list of new hobbies you wish to pursue but feel time-constrained; practice making minor adjustments to your schedule. Identify opportunities to allocate five minutes and commence with that.

- Identify aspects that can be altered by a small percentage (1 to 2 per cent) and consistently implement these changes over a few months. Consider learning a new word every day to enhance your vocabulary.

- If you enjoy reading, establish a habit of reading just one page a day or even half a page. The momentum gained will soon encourage you to read more.

- Delve into tasks you never imagined possible, such as running a marathon or climbing a mountain. Break each challenge into small, manageable parts.

- For those aspiring to adopt the habit of jogging or attending the gym but find it challenging to start, commit to keeping your shoes and workout clothes nearby. Consider this your first step.

- Often, overcoming the initial hurdle is crucial.

- Apply the 'law of least resistance' and set-up your environment to facilitate habits. For instance, if you aim to wake up early, have the tea kettle and cups ready the night before to avoid wasting time in the morning. Activation time is a significant factor.

- If you plan to write an article, start by composing the title and one line. The next time you sit down, you won't face a blank sheet; you've already made a beginning. It's a valuable initial step.

- Implement the 20-second rule: if you intend to learn a new musical instrument, keep it in plain sight to avoid wasting time searching for it and dampening your enthusiasm.
- Cultivate the habit of pausing periodically. Embrace a simple STOP practice:
  - o   S: Stop whatever you are doing
  - o   T: Take a breath and pause
  - o   O: Observe whatever is happening within you or absorb your surroundings
  - o   P: Proceed with whatever you were doing
- Develop a habit of positive emotions. Transforming positive emotions such as gratitude, kindness, awe, and others into habits is achievable, much like any other habit. Initially, engage in this consciously, and soon it will permeate every aspect of your life. Maintaining a journal for such a habit is an excellent way to monitor your progress.

AFTERWORD

$\mathcal{I}$ am standing outside the Cardiac Care Unit (CCU), waiting patiently along with other attendants for the guard to allow us to enter and visit our relatives. This is the third time in fifteen days that I had to rush back to see my mother. She seemed to be recovering well but suddenly experienced a cardiac arrest and had to be put on the ventilator. While scrolling through my WhatsApp college group, I see pictures of my friends arriving in Ooty for a reunion that was planned almost a year in advance. They tell me they are missing me, and I feel a twinge of envy on missing out on all the fun and laughter. Simultaneously, I am getting calls from the hospital and patients, reminding me of appointments and commitments. I explain my helplessness and tell them that I am not sure what the outcome is going to be and when I'll be back.

I am able to observe the various feelings running through my body—fear, despair, loss, helplessness, uncertainty, anxiety, sadness, and envy. I also sense an underlying story that is building up that I am going through a really awful phase, mummy is so sick and there is fear of losing her, and how this came at a most inappropriate time of our much-awaited get together. At the same time, there is absolute uncertainty about how things will turn out and when I'll be able to return to work and stability.

Then I realise, with a soft smile on my face, that these are stories the mind easily creates—stories of resistance, the victim card—this poor, unhappy me—non-acceptance and labelling, and interpreting reality and judging it. *How can I shift things a bit?* I ask myself.

I can simply tune into the moment and allow myself to feel what is happening *now*.

I am alive and breathing. Mummy is still alive; she is still breathing. It's a sunny, winter day, and I can see gardens, buildings, people huddled together or waiting expectantly. The warmth of the sun feels soothing on the skin. I am grateful that I can be with my mother in such a critical juncture and that she is still alive. I can allow myself to feel whatever I am feeling—anxiety, uncertainty, fear, sadness, loss, envy, hope, and gratitude.

Let me take each moment as it comes, moment by moment, hour by hour since the situation is so unpredictable that it keeps on changing. Do whatever is most appropriate for this moment. Be present with whatever is happening right now, with whatever you are feeling, surrender and allow it to be as it is. Allow things to be the way they are, the suchness and isness of things. Say yes to whatever is taking place now, say yes to whatever you are feeling right now. Allow this moment to be as it is.

I also realised with a kind of surprise that despite all the uncertainty, fear, and despair that I was feeling at the time, I also knew that at that moment nothing was really lacking. If I just remained still, I was able to see that this moment was enough, complete, and perfect. Not perfect in the way the mind envisions it, but complete and self-sufficient. Nothing more really needs to be added to it.

We need to give ourselves permission to experience the full spectrum of human emotions mindfully, with complete acceptance and non-resistance. We can lean into the experience and touch it without labels or judgement. As

Amoda Maa says, in the deepest acceptance, we meet reality as an open yes.

During interactions with people, one recurring factor was, *this* is not enough. *This* can be anything—more money, more achievements, more fame, more relations, more happiness, more spiritual progress. What I have realised through my journey is that we are never away from happiness and peace; it is our true home and refuge, and it is always where we are. Not when things improve. Things never really get sorted out; something or the other will keep coming up and create disruption. But when we completely accept whatever is happening without judgement, we come home . . . to a place of stillness and no lack. It is never away from us. To quote Voltaire, 'Wherever my travels may lead, paradise is where I am.'

Each time we get carried away by our mind and the stories it creates, we can step back, pause, and come back to the fullness of the moment. The moment as it is, in its raw form with the fullness of whatever we are experiencing. Not as we want it to be or hope it turns out to be and accept it completely.

After I completed the book and sent it for publication, by some coincidence—it's actually synchronicity—I encountered tremendous challenges in my life. One thing happened after the other, and it seemed that life had become a roller-coaster ride for me. I was discussing with a dear friend that it appeared life was challenging me to see if I could walk the talk. Could I say 'yes' to the moment, or will I become overwhelmed and lost in the content of what is happening around me? It has been through grace that I have been able to deal with the challenges, with acceptance and non-resistance. Each time I feel that I am about to get overwhelmed, I step back and pause, and remember that this is the way it is and surrender to the moment.

While I know that mindfulness and meditation may not be everyone's cup of tea, it is also not my purpose to force it on others. It will bring me great joy if people are able to take away this simple message from my book—to be present and open and engage with each moment of life as it is. It is our constant habit of wanting to choose favourable situations and reject unpleasant ones that keep us from freedom and expansiveness, which is our birthright.

It is difficult to say how all these experiences have helped me. But I can confidently say that I have become more aware and accepting; there is an abiding sense of peace that never really leaves me. Challenges come and go. The sense of peace and stillness is always there. I can tap into it whenever I feel overwhelmed. There is a moment-to-moment awareness of what is happening within me. Being aware and present brings a sense of awe and wonder to the most trivial things because there is a feeling of immense gratitude for simply being alive. And tremendous gratitude to the universe for making all this happen.

The journey continues, so do the challenges, but there is an acceptance and openness to engage with each moment fully with an open heart.

ACKNOWLEDGEMENTS

$\mathcal{I}$am indebted to my dear parents, the late Dr M. K. Dubey and Priyambada Dubey, who brought me into this world. I recently lost my mother, and I feel her presence with me during this period. This book is dedicated to their loving memory.

My biggest cheerleader has been my dearest wife and soulmate, Lopamudra (Lopa). I am especially indebted to her for giving me the space, love, and freedom to explore, search, travel, and find out the meaning of life while she remained a pillar of support for me. She has always been a source of joy, optimism, and happiness.

My daughter, Dishita, and son, Siddhartha, mean the world to me and teach me something new about life each day. My mother and father-in-law, Dr R. S. Tewari and Swati Tewari, never make me feel the lack of parents in my life and have always been there for me.

Sending a big thanks to my brother, Manoj, with whom I shared numerous beautiful memories during our growing-up years. Gratitude to my sister-in-law, Geeta, for her enduring patience and unwavering support, and to my dearly loved nephew, Manish.

I would also like to express special thanks to my sister-in-law, Gargi, brother-in-law, Naresh, and niece, Anwesha. The precious moments spent with them have created a treasure chest of memories that I hold close to my heart.

There are no words of gratitude and appreciation for my dear editor, Suma Varughese, who gave me the confidence that this book was worth reading and publishing. I will always be indebted to her for making this dream of writing a book a real possibility. I am privileged and honoured that she wrote the foreword for this book, too. She is truly a friend, philosopher, and guide to me.

A heartfelt thank you goes out to my editors, Sonali Pawar and Aditya Jarial, as well as Mr Ashok Chopra, CEO & Managing Director of Hay House Publishers, India, and the entire Hay House team. I vividly recall the euphoria upon receiving Aditya's e-mail, informing me of Hay House's interest in publishing my book. Sonali, your dedication and unwavering effort in shaping and editing this book have been truly exceptional.

Expressing gratitude to my teachers is a profound task. Many of them I have never met and may never meet in this lifetime, yet their words and writings have touched my being and transformed my life in countless ways. Eckhart Tolle ignited my journey to presence and self-discovery the very first time I set eyes on his book. Every word in his books and talks has been a treasure guiding me along this transformative path.

My heartfelt gratitude goes out to dear Mooji, Rupert Spira, and Adyashanti for the profound transformation they've brought into my life. I owe a deep debt of gratitude to Anantaji (Father) for his love, wisdom, guidance, and the endorsement of this book. I express my thanks to Swami Sarvapriyananda, Sadhguru Jaggi Vasudeva, Sri M, Mark Nepo, Tara Brach, David Bingham, Deepak Chopra, Brené Brown, Elizabeth Gilbert, Elizabeth Lesser, Tami Simon, Jay Shetty, Oprah Winfrey, Hugh Delehanty, Alan Seale, Janice

Marturano, and Dr Abraham Verghese—whose writings have been profoundly powerful and transformative.

A special moment of gratitude for all my academic teachers, with sincere thanks to Prof. S. K. Sarin and Dr Nirmal Kumar, my mentors. I am indebted to Prof. A. S. Puri and Prof. B.C. Sharma for their invaluable training and guidance in the field of Gastroenterology. My thanks extend to Dr Ajay Kumar for his unwavering support and wisdom over the years, along with his generous endorsement of the book. To all my teachers who have played a role in shaping my life, I am truly grateful.

A big thank you to Alan Seale, Hugh Delehanty, David Bingham, and Dr Reena Kotecha for their generous endorsement of my book. A special thank you to Dr Sujata Sharma, who is a prolific author and dear friend, for her generous words and appreciation. I am really grateful to my friend and author Ajay Kalra for his brilliant suggestions and endorsement.

I wish to express my deepest gratitude to my dear childhood friend Samudra Bhattacharya for all the unconditional help he has extended towards the book. A heartfelt appreciation to my dear friends, including Dr Naresh Agarwal, with whom I've shared countless discussions about life. Gratitude to Dr Rajashekhar Reddi, Dr Sanjay Garg, Rajiv Singh, Rashi Kumar, Samiksha, Neeta, Dr Basab Mukherji, Dr Priya Macaden, Dr Sanjeev Maskara, Dr Sunil Zachariah, Dr Indu Koshi, Dr Anindita Roy, Dr Shakuntala Ghosh, Dr Swati Chavda, Dr Amitabh David Singh, Dr Sridhar Prasad, and many others who have played a significant role in shaping and enriching my life. Special thanks to Sumit Sanyal for consistently engaging me in stimulating discussions. I also want to express my profound appreciation to my friend and author, Sapna Narayan, for providing invaluable guidance on shaping this book.

Expressing appreciation to my cherished friend Raj Kumar, with whom I've experienced numerous retreats and engaging conversations. Grateful to Ravi bhai, Shankarji, Girishji, and Rohini ji for their valuable wisdom and guidance. Special thanks to Sumehar and Shweta for the delightful company.

I extend my gratitude to my ever-supportive neighbours and friends, Shikha and Prashant, who have consistently been there for my family. A heartfelt thank you to the entire Batch of 90 at CMC Vellore, a significant pillar of support and friendship throughout my life. I express my appreciation to the friends from Loyola School Jamshedpur, as well as all my colleagues and seniors from the Gastro department of GB Pant Hospital, Delhi.

A big thank you to my colleagues and friends at Kailash Hospital Noida, who have been integral to my life and work over the past 15 years, with special mention to Dr Mahesh Sharma, Dr Uma Sharma, Dr Gurnani, and many others.

Lastly, I am grateful to the Universe and Life itself, which has imparted me numerous lessons and presented both setbacks and tools of resilience. Thank you for all the challenges and moments of breaking apart, as they have helped me discover who I truly am.

BIBLIOGRAPHY

Achor, Shawn. *The Happiness Advantage: The Seven Principles that Fuel Success and Performance at Work*. New York: Penguin Random House, 2010.

Ardagh, Arjuna. *Radical Brilliance: The Anatomy of How and Why People Have Original Life-changing ideas*. SelfXPress, Kindle.

Babauta, Leo. 'The Ridiculously Awesome Practice of Surrendering.' Zen Habits. Accessed 11 November 2023, www.zenhabits.net.

Bach, Tara. 'Transforming Two Fears: FOF and FOMO.' March 24, 2021. https://youtu.be/pXNEM4wjSmE

Bain, Barnet. *The Book of Doing and Being: Rediscovering Creativity in Life, Love, and Work*. New York: Atria, 2015.

Bindra, Abhinav. 'Lot of People Suffer from Mental Crisis Trying to Handle Failure, in My Case, It Was Success.' *The Indian Express*, March 13, 2021.

Brach, Tara. 'Living with Courageous Presence.' February 9, 2019. https://www.tarabrach.com/courageous-presence/

Brenner, Gail. *The End of Self-Help*. USA: Ananda Press, 2015. Kindle.

Brown, Brené. *Daring Greatly: How the Courage to Be Vulnerable Transforms the Way We Live, Love, Parent, and Lead*. New York: Gotham Books, 2012.

Bryant, Fred B., Veroff, Joseph. *Savoring: A New Model of Positive Experience*. New York: Psychology Press, 2007.

Burch, Vidyamala. *Living Well with Pain and Illness*. Colorado: Sounds True, 2010.

Byrne, Rhonda. *The Greatest Secret*. London: Thorsons, 2020. Kindle.

Cameron, Kim, et al. 'Effects of Positive Practices on Organizational Effectiveness.' *Journal of Applied Behavioral Sciences* 47, no. 3 (2011): 266–308.

Chödrön, Pema. *The Places That Scare You*. Massachusetts: Element, 2013. Kindle.

Chödrön, Pema. *Welcoming the Unwelcome: Wholehearted Living in a Brokenhearted World*. Colorado: Shambhala Publications, 2019.

Chödrön, Pema. *When Things Fall Apart: Heart Advice for Difficult Times*. Massachusetts: Element, 2013. Kindle.

Clear, James. *Atomic Habits: An Easy and Proven Way to Build Good Habits and Break Bad Ones*. New York: Avery, 2018.

Colzato, L.S., Oztruck, A., and Hommel, B. 'Meditate to Create: The Impact of Focused-Attention and Open Monitoring Training on Convergent and Divergent Thinking.' *Frontiers in Psychology*, 2 April 18:3:116, 2012.

Davis, Jeffrey. *Tracking Wonder: Reclaiming a Life of Meaning and Possibility in a World Obsessed with Productivity*. Colorado: Sounds True, 2021.

Dwoskin, Hale. 'Thoughts Don't Think.' Podcast 'Letting Go and the Greatest Secret,' Aug 30, 2021.

Eagle, Jack and Amster, Michael. *The Power of Awe*. London: Yellow Kite, 2023.

Fehmi, Les and Robbins, Jim. *The Open Focus Brain: Harvesting the Power of Attention to Heal Mind and Body*. Colorado: Shambhala Publications, 2007.

Fogg, B.J. *Tiny Habits: Why Starting Small Makes Lasting Change Easy*. London: Penguin Random House.

Foreman, Chad. 'The Incredible Mind-Altering Meditation of Sky Gazing and How to Do It.' *The Way of Meditation*, 9 December 2015.

Foster, Jeff. 'When You Stop Running Away.' lifewithoutcentre.com, October 1, 2018.

Fredrickson, Barbara. *Positivity: Groundbreaking Research to Release Your Inner Optimist and Thrive.* Oxford: One World Publications, 2010. Kindle.

Gelb, J. Michael. *How to Think Like Leonardo da Vinci.* New York: Penguin Random House, 1998.

Gilbert, Elizabeth. *Big Magic: Creativity Living Beyond Fear.* New York: Penguin Random House, 2015.

Glenie, Evelyn. 'How to Truly Listen.' March 14, 2007, YouTube.

Goleman, Tara Bennet. *Emotional Alchemy.* New York: Harmony Books, 2001. Kindle.

Goleman-Bennet, Tara. *Mind Whispering: A New Map to Freedom from Self-Defeating Emotional Habits.* New York: Harper Collins.

Goode, Greg. *Standing as Awareness: The Direct Path.* Bath, UK: Non-Duality Press, 2009.

Greenspan, Miriam. *Healing through the Dark Emotions: The Wisdom of Grief, Fear, and Despair.* Colorado: Shambhala Publications, 2004. Kindle.

Hanson, Rick. *Hardwiring Happiness: How to Reshape Your Brain and Your Life.* London: Ebury Digital, 2013. Kindle.

Harding, Douglas. *Face to No-Face: Rediscovering Our Original Nature.* North Carolina: Lulu Press, 2020. Kindle.

Harding, Kelli. *The Rabbit Effect: Live Longer, Happier and Healthier by the Groundbreaking Science of Kindness.* New York: Atria Books, 2019.

Hendricks, Gay. *The Big Leap: Conquer Your Hidden Fear and Take Life to the Next Level.* San Francisco: HarperOne, 2009.

Hill, Austin Shaw. 'Creativity Matters: Mission.' Accessed 11 November 2023, https://austinhillshaw.com/.

Hougaard, Rasmus, et al. 'Mindful Leadership: Achieving Results by Managing the Mind.' *Leader to Leader,* 2016(79): 49–56.

Joyce, James. *Dubliners—A Painful Case.* London: Grant Richards, 1914.

Juster, Norton. *The Phantom Tollbooth.* London: Harper Collins, 1961. Kindle.

Kaufman, A. Keith. *Mindful Sport Performance Enhancement: Mental Training for Athletes and Coaches.* Washington D. C.: American Psychological Association, 2017. Kindle.

Kelly, Loch. *Shift into Freedom: The Science and Practice of Open-Hearted Awareness.* Colorado: Sounds True, 2015.

Keltner, Dacher. *The Transformative Power of Everyday Wonder.* London: Allen Lane, 2023.

Killingsworth, A. Mathew, Gilbert, T. Daniel. 'A Wandering Mind is an Unhappy Mind.' *Science,* 330, 932 (2010).

Kiloby, Scott. *Natural Rest for Addiction: A Revolutionary Way to Recover Through Presence.* Bath, UK: Non-Duality Press, 2017.

Kirsten, Neff Dr. 'Self-Compassion and 3 Components of Self-Compassion.' www.self-compassion.org.

Kotler, Steve. *The Art of Impossible: A Peak Performance Primer.* San Francisco: HarperOne, 2021.

Kukk, Christopher L. *The Compassionate Achiever: How Helping Others Fuels Success.* San Francisco: HarperOne, 2017.

Lesser, Elizabeth. *Broken Open: How Difficult Times Can Help Us Grow.* New York: Random House, 2004.

Lorde, Audre. 'The Transformation of Silence into Action and Language.'

Lyubomirsky, Sonja. *The How of Happiness.* New York: Penguin Books, 2007.

Maa, Amoda. 'The Jewel within the Darkness.' March 23, 2022. Blog.

Maa, Amoda. *Embodied Enlightenment: Living Your Awakening in Every Moment.* CA: New Harbinger, 2017.

Macarthur, Robin Marie. 'The Courage to Write: On the Radical Generosity of Letting Yourself Be Seen.' January 28, 2022 (Literary Hub).

Marturano, Janice. *Finding the Space to Lead: A Practical Guide to Mindful Leadership.* New York: Bloomsbury Press, 2014.

Masters, Robert. *Emotional Intimacy: A Comprehensive Guide for Connecting with the Power of Your Emotions.* Colorado: Sounds True, 2013. Kindle.

Mecking, Olga. *Niksen: Embracing the Dutch Art of Doing Nothing.* London: Piatkus, 2010.

Meena Srinivasan. *Teach, Breathe, Learn: Mindfulness In and Out of the Classroom.* CA: Parallax Press, 2014.

Nepo, Mark. *Finding Inner Courage.* Oregon: Heron Books, 2012.

Ostafin, B. D. and Kassman, K. T. 'Stepping out of History: Mindfulness Improves Insight Problem Solving.' *Consciousness and Cognition,* 21, 2012, pp. 1031–6.

Ostaseski, Frank. *The Five Invitations: Discovering What Death Can Teach Us About Living Fully.* New York: Flatiron Books, 2017.

Palmer, Parker. 'The Gift of Presence: The Perils of Advice.' On Being with Krista Tippet.

Paquette, Jonah. *Awestruck: How Embracing Wonder Can Make You Happier, Healthier, and More Connected.* Colorado: Shambhala Publications, 2020.

Pema Chödrön. *When Things Fall Apart: Heart Advice for Difficult Times.* Colorado: Shambhala Publications, 1996.

Penman, Danny Dr. *Mindfulness for Creativity: Adapt, Create and Thrive in a Frantic World.* London: Piatkus, 2015.

Phil Jackson and Hugh Delehanty. *Eleven Rings.* New York: Penguin Press, 2013.

Plett, Heather. *The Art of Holding Space: A Practice of Love, Liberation, and Leadership.* Vancouver: Page Two, 2020.

Prendergast, J. John. *The Deep Heart: Our Portal to Presence.* Colorado: Sounds True, 2019.

Rinpoche, Ponlop. *Emotional Rescue: How to Work with Your Emotions to Transform Hurt and Confusion into Energy That Empowers You.* New York: Penguin Random House, 2016.

Rome, I. David. *Your Body Knows the Answer.* Boston: Shambhala Publications, 2014.

Rosenberg, Joan. *90 Seconds to a Life You Love: How to Turn Difficult Feelings into Rock Solid Confidence.* London: Yellow Kite, 2022.

Rubin, Jeffrey. Foreword to Cacciatore Joanne. *Bearing the Unbearable.* Somerville, MA: Wisdom Publications, 2017.

Seligman, Martin. *Flourish: A New Understanding of Happiness and Well-Being.* London: Nicholas Brealey Publishing, 2011.

Seppala, Emma. *The Happiness Track: How to Apply the Science of Happiness to Accelerate Your Success.* New York: HarperOne, 2016.

Sharma, Robin. *The Monk Who Sold His Ferrari.* San Francisco: Harper, 1999.

Sharma, Sujata. *A Dragonfly's Purpose.* Chennai: Notion Press, 2019.

Shiota, Michelle. 'Awe, Wonder, and the Human Mind' in *Annals of the New York Academy of Sciences,* March 4, 2021.

Singer, Michael A. *The Surrender Experiment: My Journey into Life's Perfection.* London: Yellow Kite, 2015.

Sounds True: *Insights at the Edge* - Google Podcast. Tami Simon and Mark Nepo.

Spira, Rupert. *You Are the Happiness You Seek.* Oxford: Sahaja Publications, 2018.

Taylore, Jill Bolte. *My Stroke of Insight: A Brain Scientist's Personal Journey.* London: Hodder and Stoughton Ltd, 2006.

The Work of Byron Katie. www.thework.com

Tolle, Eckhart. *A New Earth: Create a Better Life.* London: Penguin Books, 2009.

Tolle, Eckhart. *The Power of Now.* CA: New World Library, 2004.

Wahba, Orly. *Kindness Boomerang: How to Save the World Through 365 Daily Acts.* New York: Flatiron Books, 2017.